KNIFE FIGHTING
A Practical Course

KNIFE FIGHTING
A Practical Course

Michael D. Janich

PALADIN PRESS • BOULDER, COLORADO

Other books by Michael Janich

Blowguns: The Breath of Death

Bullseyes Don't Shoot Back: The Complete Textbook of Point
Shooting for Close Quarters Combat (with Col. Rex Applegate)

Street Steel: Choosing and Carrying Self-Defense Knives

Knife Fighting:
A Practical Course
by Michael D. Janich

Copyright © 1993 by Michael D. Janich

ISBN 0-87364-740-8
Printed in the United States of America

Published by Paladin Press, a division of
Paladin Enterprises, Inc., P.O. Box 1307,
Boulder, Colorado 80306, USA.
(303) 443-7250

Direct inquiries and/or orders to the above address.

PALADIN, PALADIN PRESS, and the "horse head" design
are trademarks belonging to Paladin Enterprises and
registered in United States Patent and Trademark Office.

Contents

Warning

The techniques and drills depicted in this book are extremely dangerous. The author and publisher disclaim any liability from any damage or injuries that a user of this book may suffer, as well as any liability from any damage or injuries to third parties from the user of this book. This book is *for informational purposes only.*

Introduction

uring the past several years, interest in the subject of knife fighting has enjoyed a tremendous resurgence. Increasing street crime has made people more aware of their vulnerability to becoming victims of attacks. The realization by many members of society that they, not the police, are primarily responsible for their own defense has prompted many of them to seek a means of self-defense. Some have purchased guns to defend themselves in their homes, but most are still unwilling or unable to go out in public carrying a firearm. For economic, utilitarian, and other reasons, the knife has become the compromise weapon of choice for many.

Within the martial arts community, the widespread exposure of the Filipino martial arts, in which use of edged weapons is quite prevalent, has also helped promote interest in knife fighting and given it credibility as a viable martial arts pursuit.

The increasing number and notoriety of craftsmen who make custom knives by hand has also helped. Most of these craftsmen offer at least one style of combat knife, and many specialize in fighting and self-defense knives. Commercial cutlery companies that had previously produced only utilitarian and hunting designs have also begun introducing knives that are unmistakably intended for use as weapons. Several new commercial companies have entered the market and built thriving businesses by producing fighting knives exclusively.

One symptom, as well as a part of the cause, of this renewed interest in knife fighting has been the publication of a number of books on the subject. The authors of these books have ranged from Special Forces veterans to reform school alumni to ex-convicts. The fact that you are reading this particular book may mean that you have read some of the others. I have. It may also mean that you're wondering what I have to say about knife fighting that hasn't already been said. The answer is, a lot.

For the past 16 years, I have studied knife fighting with a number of instructors and trained with police, members of the U.S. Special Forces, and street fighters, in addition to reading everything I could find on the subject of knife fighting. Through these efforts, I have become proficient at fighting with a knife. I also realized that, although almost all of the books available concerning this subject offer some information of value, there was no publication that actually provided methodical instruction in knife fighting that would allow a novice knife fighter to develop a reasonable degree of skill. Some offered bits of useful information and a history of the art but failed to provide comprehensive instruction. Others demonstrated numerous individual techniques but never explained the concepts behind them. Still others did nothing more than criticize the teachings of other authors.

My objective in writing this book is to provide the average martial artist, soldier, or self-defense-minded citizen with *systematic* instruction in the fundamentals of fighting with a knife. It is my hope that a person wishing to acquire the skills to fight with a knife can read this book and, by grasping the concepts presented herein and seriously practicing their application, become a proficient knife fighter. I do not claim that this is the ultimate work on knife fighting, but I believe it fills a gap that other materials haven't.

At times in this book, I do criticize the teachings of others. This is not done to make my book or my techniques look better at the expense of someone else's. The intent is to alert you to a technique or practice that is dangerous to *you* and should be avoided at all costs. You don't want to wait to realize that a practice is unsound until you're staring at your knife on the ground in front of you and trying to push your intestines back into your body with your hands.

If you are truly interested in becoming a skilled knife fighter, I recommend that you read everything you can find on the subject, watch instructional videos, seek out instruction from recognized martial artists, practice regularly with a partner (a variety of partners is even better), and ultimately decide what works best for you. Knife fighting is a martial art. A martial art, like any other art, is a means of self-expression. Two painters can be given an identical set of paints and brushes and receive identical instruction in the fundamentals of painting. However, if they are each given a canvas and asked to paint, the resulting pictures will be different. Each artist will interpret the instruction he received and apply it, *taking advantage of his own particular talents*. The results will be different, but neither will be more "right" than the other. The important thing is to obtain the desired result.

Similarly, each reader of this book will find certain techniques particularly suitable to his stature, physical condition, and abilities. Concentrate on grasping the principles and concepts presented in this book and develop them to suit your personal style. Remember that the combative techniques shown in the photos are only examples based on the concepts. Each technique shown is one way of dealing with a specific situation, but it is by no means the only way. Practice the techniques, but don't be afraid to modify them to make them work better for you.

There are some who would argue that this book should not have been published because the information herein could be used by criminals, gang members, and their ilk. Many of the people who would offer this argument would have been far better qualified to write this book than I, but continue to selfishly guard their knowledge, offering it only to a select few. My response to them is that I believe providing the average citizen with an adequate means of defending himself is more important than the fear that the literate minority of the miscreants who endanger our society might get a little more dangerous. My advice to the reader is to be aware of this possibility and *practice even harder than the criminals and gang members*! Most of them are looking for victims, not challenges. They will not continue an assault if confronted by a confident, determined opponent armed with a sharp knife and the knowledge to use it effectively.

CHAPTER ONE

Some Thoughts on Knife Fighting

Before discussing the actual physical techniques and tactics of knife fighting, a few general comments are in order.

THE FIRST RULE: AVOID IF POSSIBLE

The first rule of knife fighting is, unless it is impossible to avoid it, *don't do it*! A sharp knife is an extremely dangerous and unpredictable weapon. People who carry knives and whom you are likely to confront in a knife fight are also often dangerous and unpredictable. If you can possibly avoid a confrontation, do so. Walk, run, or drive away and diffuse the situation before it escalates.

EXPECT TO GET CUT

If you have no choice and are forced to face an opponent armed with a blade, expect to get cut. If you prepare yourself mentally before hand with the thought that you will most likely get cut, you will reduce the psychological shock you will suffer if it does happen. Psychological shock can be every bit as crippling as the shock caused by physical injury. The perception that you have suffered a serious injury can convince your body to react as if you had, even if the injury is a minor one. But if you accept that you will probably be cut and prepare mentally for the effects, you can overcome them and continue the fight.

DON'T FORGET YOUR OTHER WEAPONS

Although knife fighting by definition is concerned primarily with the techniques of applying the knife as a weapon, it does not and should not limit your techniques to those involving the knife alone. In other words, just because you have a knife in your hand, don't become so fixated on it that you forget the other weapons at your disposal. Your free hand, for example, can be used not only for blocking, checking, and grabbing, it can also administer a variety of offensive strikes that can create openings for your knife or may even end the fight altogether. A good repertoire of *practical* kicks can also be used to create or maintain distance from your opponent, to open him up for knife attacks, or to take him out of the fight completely by destroying his foundation (if he can't stand, he can't fight). The point is that a knife should complement your existing arsenal of body weapons, not replace it.

In a knife fight, use whatever weapons you have available and don't become fixated on your knife. It should complement your natural body weapons, not replace them. Knife fighting is a total body endeavor.

DEGREES OF FORCE

The knife is a weapon that can be applied with a tremendous range of force. It need not be considered a tool of maximum (i.e., lethal) force, but in your training you should always apply it as such. *Practice every technique with the intent of following through to the death of your opponent.*

In some cases, the mere sight of a shiny blade in your hand can be enough to discourage a potential attacker, effectively ending a fight before it starts. If your opponent is intent upon attacking you, a solid offensive or defensive cut to his hand or arm could be enough to make him rethink his intentions and quit the fight. The unfortunate thing is that different attackers can react in different ways. A hand cut that would force one attacker to drop his knife and run might enrage another attacker and make him even more determined.

In a real confrontation, you will have to decide how far you want to go with your technique based on the circumstances. If you've just severed all the tendons in your attacker's hand and he is obviously unable and unwilling to continue the fight, you may decide that there is no need to inflict further injury and break contact. You cannot assume, however, that a solid cut will always elicit that same response. You must be ready and willing to continue your technique through to the end. If you've trained to do this, when the situation warrants and it is necessary to do so, you will be able to do it without hesitation. If, in your practice sessions, you always stop short or finish your techniques without conviction, you may hesitate to follow through in a real situation. That moment of hesitation can be enough to kill you. *Practice like it's for real, because at any time it might be!*

The scenarios in which you might use your knife as a defensive weapon are many. They can include defending yourself against larger or multiple unarmed opponents, or attackers armed with various weapons. The typical use of knife fighting skills that most people envision, however, has two combatants armed with knives facing each other *West Side Story*-style. Although this is not an impossible occurrence, it is not necessarily the most probable, either.

Most people with any amount of common sense will try to avoid such a situation by walking or running away. If you are unable to flee the area and have no choice but to face a man armed with a knife, your first act should be to look for a superior weapon. *Only when all reasonable alternatives have been exhausted should you consider facing a man knife against knife.*

MORAL DECISIONS

Assuming that you have no other choice and you find yourself, knife in hand, facing someone who is also armed with a knife or other deadly weapon, you have already made the decision that you are going to fight for your life. Likewise, you have also made the decision that you might have to kill your opponent to ensure your own survival. These decisions must have been made long before that moment and any moral reservations you might have about those decisions worked out to your own satisfaction. If they haven't been, your chances of survival will be significantly diminished.

THE BEST DEFENSE IS A GOOD OFFENSE

Again, assuming this situation and the foregone conclusions that it brings, do not restrict yourself to a defensive role. *Attack your attacker!* You, as the law-abiding citizen in this scenario, have already been pushed beyond the reasonable limits of constraint and are facing an armed opponent. Don't wait for him to attack so you can defend yourself. The fact that you are standing there in that situation means that you are already in fear for your life. You don't need any more provocation than that. If you attack aggressively and draw first blood, you may be able to end the confrontation quickly or "slash and dash," cutting him and then beating a hasty retreat. If he chooses to continue the fight, your first cut

should have at least caused some damage that will make him less effective and your subsequent strikes a bit easier to land.

When forced into a situation where you find yourself facing an armed opponent, don't wait for him to attack to defend yourself. Attack your attacker!

LEGAL CONSIDERATIONS

You may be thinking that by taking the above course of action and striking first, the twisted nature of our legal system might make you the aggressor if the incident were ever tried in court. Unfortunately, this is true. However, it presupposes that 1) your opponent survives to try to press charges against you, and 2) your opponent is willing to contact the police and risk prosecution himself. Again, you must make your own moral decisions, apply the amount of force you deem appropriate for the situation at hand, and decide how you want to deal with the consequences of your actions. If you ultimately do end up in court, at least you'll do it alive. The old adage, "I'd rather be tried by twelve than carried by six" still rings true.

The bottom line is, if you're going to carry a knife, develop the confidence and attitude to use it skillfully and the wisdom and judgment to keep from using it unless you absolutely have to.

CHAPTER TWO

Grip

T he most basic, yet least understood, aspect of knife fighting is the grip. The grip you take on your fighting knife is your link to it as a weapon. It will not only determine how effectively you can employ your knife in a fight, it is what protects you from injuring your own hand when you make contact with a target. A proper grip will ensure that all your cuts and thrusts will transfer the maximum amount of force into your target, while allowing you to maintain complete control of your blade. At the same time, it will allow your hand to absorb any shock transmitted back through the knife handle without injury.

Most knife-fighting books written in recent years, when discussing knife grips, rehash information originally published in World War II close combat manuals (e.g., Col. Rex Applegate's *Kill or Get Killed*). They describe in great detail the pros and cons of the "hammer grip," "saber grip," "foil grip," and "ice-pick grip," but ultimately do little to add to the reader's understanding of what constitutes a good grip on a knife.

SABER GRIP

The most often taught fighting grip is the saber grip, so named because of its similarity to the grip taken on a fencing saber. The knife handle is laid diagonally across the palm, and the fingers are curled naturally around it. The thumb is positioned directly on top of the handle or slightly to the left of center (for a right-hand grip). The focus of the hand's grasp is concentrated in the index and middle fingers and the thumb, while the ring and little fingers provide additional support and leverage. The wrist is turned downward and locked to aim the point of the knife directly at the target.

will try to continue on. The result will be that your thumb and index finger will be forcefully driven into the knife guard, severely bruising them and quite possibly disabling that hand. If you are using a knife without a guard, your hand would continue forward onto the blade of the knife, cutting your fingers and possibly the tendons that enable you to grip the weapon. Even if you survive the rest of the encounter, you might lose the function of that hand permanently. If you were able to maintain your grip and keep your hand on the handle of the knife, the shock of your strike would be absorbed by your wrist. The fact that the saber grip requires that your wrist be turned downward at an

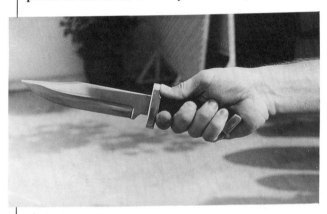 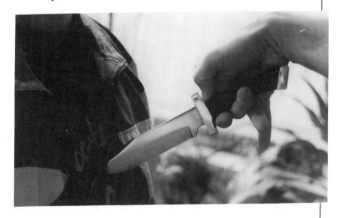

The saber grip is the most commonly taught knife-fighting grip. Although it looks practical and functional, its shortcomings become painfully obvious when you make hard contact.

Although the saber grip is considered by many to be the ideal knife grip, this is only true if you never make hard contact with your target. If you ever do, the deficiencies of this grip will become painfully obvious.

First, if you make a hard slashing stroke and happen to hit a bony target, it is likely that the knife will come loose in your hand or that you will drop it altogether. The same is also true if you should happen to smash knuckles with your opponent when attempting to cut his knife hand. The reason for this is that the grip's pressure is focused on the relatively small area of two fingers and the ball of the thumb.

The disadvantages of this grip will be even more apparent if you attempt a forceful thrust with your knife and hit a resilient target (bone, heavy clothing, jewelry, pocket contents, etc.). Your blade will stop but the hand propelling it

unnatural angle in order to execute a thrust would leave it vulnerable to being sprained, again preventing you from continuing the fight.

Assuming that you have a grip of steel and are not susceptible to the problems described above, the saber grip still falls short as a fighting grip. The reason is that it does not allow you to strike at a target quickly and instinctively with any degree of accuracy. Try this test: using a Magic Marker or a piece of masking tape, make a small mark about an inch in diameter on the side of a cardboard box. Place the box on a support or hang it by a cord so it's about chest to head level. With your favorite fighting knife held in a saber grip, stand about three feet from your target. Now, as quickly as you can, thrust at the target, aiming for the mark you made. Repeat the process about a dozen times and you'll soon realize that it's very difficult to hit the mark. If you try this test with knives of different sizes, you'll find that it's even more difficult to thrust accurately with long-bladed knives than with short-bladed ones.

FILIPINO GRIP

If the saber grip is not the ideal fighting grip, what is? The answer comes from the Filipino martial arts, so I have termed it simply the Filipino grip. Knife fighting figures prominently in all the Filipino martial arts and is deeply rooted in Filipino martial tradition. Instructors of the Filipino arts of *escrima*, *kali*, and *arnis de mano* are usually highly trained in knife techniques. Unfortunately, they are also usually unwilling to teach knife techniques to anyone but their most senior students. This practice does allow them to screen the people to whom they impart this knowledge, but also keeps these skills out of the hands of the many respectable martial artists and other individuals having a legitimate need to defend themselves. As you'll see as you read this book, my objective is to provide as much knowledge as possible so you can develop a

functional level of knife-fighting skill in the quickest possible time. How you use the skills you develop is up to you, and you alone will bear responsibility for your actions.

To assume a proper Filipino grip, lay the handle of your knife across your palm at the base of your fingers. Curl all four fingers naturally around the handle, but concentrate the pressure of your grasp on the middle, ring, and little fingers. The idea is to use these fingers to anchor the lower half of the handle into your palm. The index finger is curled loosely around the handle and the thumb is extended parallel to the blade. Your wrist should remain in a natural position so the blade and your thumb are at about a 120-degree angle to your forearm.

The Filipino grip offers a number of advantages over the saber grip. By focusing the grip on the last three fingers of the hand, you increase the area of your hand that is firmly in contact with the handle of the knife and anchor it securely into your palm. In this way, the shock of a hard strike is absorbed by the meaty flesh of your palm, preventing injury and allowing you to maintain control of your knife. The increased contact area also ensures that your

The Filipino grip is a much more practical grip for knife fighting. To assume this grip, lay the handle of your knife across your palm. Curl the last three fingers of your hand tightly around the base of the handle. This is the focus of pressure for the grip and anchors the handle of the knife securely to your palm. Then curl the index finger lightly around the handle and extend your thumb parallel to the blade. The knife in these photos is a bowie handmade by the author.

hand will not slide toward the blade during a powerful thrust. This allows you to apply full-force thrusts with knives equipped with guards without fearing injury to your hand. It also allows you to use effectively the small guard-less boot knives and folding knives that are popular for self-defense carry today.

The natural angle of the wrist when using the Filipino grip provides two advantages: it allows the wrist to absorb the shock of strikes without injury, and it presents an ideal engagement angle for the blade to cut during slashes. What this means is that, because the blade is held at an angle to your forearm, during a slashing motion, its edge will strike the target at an angle. This allows more linear surface of the edge to contact the target and results in the blade being drawn through the target rather than chopped into it. The more edge surface that comes in contact with your target, the deeper you will cut.

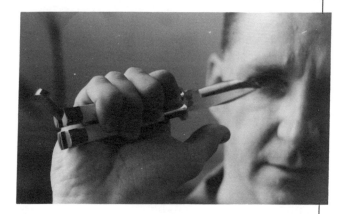

This photo shows how, with the Filipino grip, the thumb of the knife hand instinctively guides the blade to the target. This grip is often seen used by Filipino martial artists, but it is never explained.

The natural wrist angle of the Filipino grip protects the wrist from injury during hard contact and places the angle in an ideal engagement position during slashes. This angle ensures that the full length of the blade edge is drawn through the target, guaranteeing a deep cut.

The greatest advantage of the Filipino grip is that it allows you to use your established neuromuscular pathways to guide your blade to the desired target instinctively. This is where the extended thumb comes into play. If you have ever read any articles on the Filipino martial arts or seen a trained *escrima* practitioner wield a knife, you may have noticed he kept the thumb of his knife hand extended. The reason for this is that the thumb acts as a guide or a pointer to lead the knife to its target.

From the time we were very small, we have been developing our eye-hand and eye-finger coordination. We began by learning such simple actions as sticking our thumbs into our mouths and gradually developed the ability to almost instinctively execute precise, coordinated movements. For example, it is quite natural and easy for a normal adult to press a door bell or push a button quickly. It does not require extensive thought or calculation because the neuromuscular pathways that allow such a movement have been finely tuned during years of performing such simple movements.

Remember the test you did trying to thrust at a small target with a knife held in the saber grip? Let's try it again, but a bit differently. With your target set up as before, stand in front of it with your hands empty. As quickly as you can, jab your thumb at the mark on your target. The technique you want to use is to make a loose fist but leave your thumb extended. As you extend your arm toward the target, turn your fist palm up and hit with the tip of your thumb. You'll probably have no difficulty hitting very near or right on your mark.

Now pick up your knife and hold it in the Filipino grip with your thumb extended just above and parallel to the blade. Without thinking of the knife, thrust your thumb at the mark again. You'll find the point of your knife stuck in or very near the mark on the target. Your natural ability to hit the target with your thumb automatically allows you to hit accurately with the point of the blade.

The natural indexing ability of your thumb also allows you to slash with great precision by using the Filipino grip. Instead of using a thrusting motion, imagine that you are wiping the ball of your thumb across the target. The edge of the blade, being aligned on the same plane as your thumb, will strike the target where your thumb was aimed.

To ensure that you maintain full control of your knife and prevent injury to your thumb, always curl it in at the instant you make contact with your target. This provides an even more secure grip and keeps your thumb out of harm's way as your blade does its work.

REVERSE OR ICE-PICK GRIP

The standard Filipino grip is the recommended grip for the stereotypical knife fight, where both opponents know that the other is armed and they face each other head on. In other circumstances, it might be advisable to conceal the fact that you are armed to give you the advantage of surprise. The best way to do this is by using the reverse or ice-pick grip. This grip is assumed in exactly the same was as the Filipino grip, but the knife is reversed 180 degrees so the blade protrudes from the little-finger side of the hand. Held in this way, the wrist can be rotated to conceal the blade behind the forearm. From that position, it can be used for a surprise offensive attack in response to your opponent's threat or for a variety of defensive techniques. The use of the extended thumb as a guide still works with the

reverse grip, but it must be adjusted. The thrusting motion of the tip of the thumb is now used to guide the blade during cutting motions. The thumb is aimed just past the target so the blade edge that follows it will strike. The wiping action of the ball of the thumb will guide thrusts with the point of the knife. In this case, the thumb never reaches the target as the point of the knife strikes first.

It should be noted that some instructors teach the reverse grip as the preferred grip for face-to-face knife-fighting encounters. I do not agree with this practice because it shortens your reach and limits your offensive techniques, placing you in a primarily defensive role. Knife fighting is an *offensive* proposition. Attack your attacker!

The reverse grip is useful in some situations but is generally less desirable than the Filipino grip because it places you in a primarily defensive position. The advantages of this grip include being able to conceal the knife behind your wrist and being able to hook and trap with the blade.

CHAPTER THREE

Stance

In addition to a proper grip, a good stance is necessary in order to be an effective knife fighter. The stance you take will determine how quickly and effectively you can attack as well as how vulnerable you will be to your opponent's attacks. It will also determine how well you will be able to move to get in and out of contact range.

ELEMENTS OF PROPER STANCE

The stance that is best suited to effective knife fighting is very similar to a traditional boxing stance, with the exception that your strong side is placed forward and your hands are held somewhat lower. This stance provides great mobility and, because the knife is in your lead hand, allows you a wide striking range. It also enables you to use all your other body weapons in conjunction with your knife, including free-hand strikes and punches, elbows, knees, and kicks. Real knife fighting is not just learning how to fight with a knife; *it is a total body endeavor*!

A good knife-fighting stance is similar to a boxer's stance, except that your strong side is forward. Your knife is held close to your body to protect it, the knees are bent, your weight is slightly forward, the rear heel is raised, the chin is tucked in, and the free hand is held with the outside of the forearm facing the opponent.

The knife-fighter's stance as seen from the side.

To assume a proper knife-fighting stance, hold your knife in your right hand (if you are naturally right-handed) and stand with your feet together. Imagine that your opponent is directly in front of you. Now take a normal step forward with your right foot. This should place your feet about shoulder-width apart.

Turn both feet slightly to the left, bend your knees, and raise your left heel slightly. Your weight should be distributed fairly evenly over both feet but should favor your front foot slightly. Keeping your weight distributed slightly forward, along with raising your rear heel, will allow you to perform explosive offensive strikes without sacrificing your backward mobility.

Your knife hand should be positioned close to your body at a level near your floating ribs.

Do not let it float out away from your body where it is vulnerable to being cut.

Raise your left hand along the left side of your neck so the back of your hand and forearm face toward your opponent. This will protect the left side of your body, neck, and head. By turning the back of your forearm out, you also protect the blood vessels and flexor tendons on the inside of your forearm. Tuck your chin in slightly and raise your right shoulder just a bit to protect the right side of your neck and throat.

What if You're Left-Handed?

If you happen to be left-handed, you will of course do the mirror image of the above instructions to assume a proper left-side-forward stance. It should be noted that most of the techniques in this book will be described and demonstrated from the perspective of a right-handed person. No offense is intended by this; it was just easier for me to do it that way since I'm naturally right-handed.

As long as we're on the subject, though, a southpaw can, of course, successfully adapt all the techniques in this book for fighting with a knife held in his left hand. If he practices against or fights another left-handed person, the techniques will be a mirror image of those demonstrated in this book. A left-handed person fighting a right-handed opponent must adapt, however, as must a natural right-hander fighting a southpaw. Adapting will be easy if you remember to learn the concepts and principles of knife fighting rather than trying to memorize individual techniques. Once you learn to react properly, you will be able to deal effectively with an opponent in any stance, striking with any type of weapon.

(While I'm at it, you'll also probably notice that I invariably choose to use the third person personal pronoun *he*. This, again, is a matter of convenience and is not intended to imply that readers of this book will be exclusively male or that only males are capable of fighting with a knife. This applies equally in those instances where I use it to refer to one's opponent, as the possibility that one's attacker will be a female certainly exists.)

Now that my disclaimers are complete, let's get back to stances.

RELAX

Once you've followed all these instructions and assumed a good knife-fighting stance, relax. The more comfortable you feel in your stance, the more easily you'll be able to move and the more quickly you'll be able to act and react. If you feel uncomfortable, check your stance because you're probably doing something wrong. Loosen the tension in your shoulders and arms and bounce lightly on the balls of your feet to develop a feeling of relaxed readiness. If you're too tense, all your actions will be slower. Speed, as you'll soon learn, is one of the best attributes of a good knife fighter.

PRACTICE UNTIL MOVEMENTS ARE INSTINCTIVE

When you feel comfortable with your stance, return to your original feet-together position and practice moving into a fighting stance. Your objective is to flow into position smoothly without having to think about all the individual elements of the stance. If you can, practice in front of a full-length mirror. Look at yourself as if you were your opponent and try to identify weaknesses in your stance. Look for obvious open targets or breaches in your defense and correct them. Practice until assuming a proper stance becomes second nature.

DISADVANTAGES OF HOLDING THE KNIFE IN YOUR REAR HAND

Some books on knife fighting criticize the practice of putting your knife hand forward, claiming that a stance with the free hand forward is superior. By keeping the knife to the rear, it is supposedly kept safe from your opponent's cuts. The idea then is to use your free hand to fend off or immobilize your opponent's knife hand, thus creating an opening for you to use your knife. Although this sounds great in theory, I have found it does not work well in practice. While you are trying to figure out how to grab your opponent's knife hand and to bring your blade into action, he can take his time and methodically carve away at your lead hand. Your knife hand, held in back,

has to travel much further to get to your opponent and has a reach disadvantage against a knife-hand-forward fighter. Even if you are extraordinarily fast, he can still cut your lead hand more quickly than you can cut his "exposed" leading knife hand. Several deep cuts to your lead arm or the loss of a few fingers would probably be enough to convince you to change your tactics.

The knife-forward stance is preferred to a stance where the free hand is placed out front. Critics' claims that putting the knife hand out front leaves it vulnerable to being cut are only true if you let it dangle out away from your body. This photo shows the difference in reach between the two stances. The knife-forward stance clearly affords superior reach.

The Exception

The only time that it is preferable to place your free hand out front and keep your knife hand back is when you have a shield of some sort in your left hand that can absorb your opponent's cuts without injury. If you are wearing a thick leather jacket when the fight starts, you might consider this. Other examples of improvised shields include garbage can lids, briefcases, and handbags.

The commonly taught trick of wrapping a jacket around your lead hand and forearm can also work, provided that you're carrying it and not wearing it at the time the fight starts. If you have enough time to take off your jacket and wrap it around your arm, you probably have enough time to beat feet and avoid the confrontation. Otherwise, you're into knife dueling and deserve what you get.

One final note, if you do choose to use this tactic, maintain an *offensive* attitude. Don't let your opponent hack away at your shield while you wait to deliver that one strike that will take him out of the fight. The longer you let a fight last, the greater the chances of your suffering a serious cut or puncture.

Use your shield to cover or immobilize your opponent's knife hand and attack his exposed targets. This usually works best if you try to push his blade downward toward his body, exposing his upper body to an attack.

CHAPTER FOUR

Footwork and Mobility

U nless you plan on all your knife fights occurring in a phone booth, your next step is to learn to move in your stance.

SIMILARITIES TO BOXING

Footwork in knife fighting is also very similar to that found in boxing. In general, it is a sliding style of movement that is initiated by the foot closest to the desired direction of travel.

Linear Movement

For example, if you want to move forward, slide your lead foot several inches forward, shift your weight forward, and slide your rear foot up to resume your original stance. To move backward, reverse the procedure so the back foot moves first and the lead foot follows.

The proper method of advancing is demonstrated here. The lead foot moves first to carry the attack to the opponent, then the rear foot follows.

Moving backward linearly is the exact opposite of advancing. The rear foot moves first, then the front foot.

Lateral Movement

For lateral movement, the same rules apply. The foot closest to the desired direction of travel moves first. If you're in a right lead stance and want to move to your left, slide your left foot several inches to the left and follow it with your right. Moving to the right is just the opposite.

Whenever you move, keep your sliding steps small and maintain your balance. Also, keep your knees bent and the level of your head basically constant. Don't jump or bounce. Sliding gives you better control and is just as fast.

Practice

As with your stance, practice your footwork in front of a mirror. When you move, don't let your stance come apart to create weaknesses that your opponent can exploit. Keep your defenses tight and maintain a relaxed readiness.

You should also practice your footwork on different surfaces to become accustomed to moving in any situation. Practice on grass, gravel, cement, tile floors, dirt, ice, snow, or any other terrain you might be likely to encounter.

Also practice both in open areas and in crowded places with lots of furniture, garbage cans, mailboxes, etc. Learn to detect these objects with your peripheral vision without taking your eyes off your opponent. Later, you'll also learn how to use these objects to your tactical advantage in a fight.

SPEED LUNGE

One type of footwork that is effective when making offensive cuts was originally borrowed from fencing but was used most in the point (noncontact) karate arena. For lack of a better name, I call it the speed lunge.

Unlike the long, exaggerated lunges seen in formal fencing, this is a quick, economical movement that allows you to strike and close with your opponent with tremendous speed. Notice that I specified strike then close, in that order.

This technique became popular among the better tournament karate competitors because it allowed them to hit their opponents with great speed. Point karate, unlike full-contact karate, does not require hard contact for the person performing a technique to win a point. Light contact or, in some cases, near contact is all that's needed for the judge to award a point. If, during a clash, both opponents score, the one who scored first gets the point. To take advantage of this scoring system, tournament competitors developed footwork that allowed them to hit very quickly, literally "beating their opponent to the punch" to get points.

Speed was the primary concern and was often attained at the expense of power. This would not necessarily be a good trade-off in an unarmed encounter but makes perfect sense in knife fighting. It doesn't take that much power to inflict a deep cut with a knife.

To perform the footwork for the speed lunge, first assume your guard stance. Remember that your weight should be slightly forward, your knees bent, and your rear heel raised. Now, *without shifting your weight to the rear*, quickly raise your lead foot and try to touch it to the inside of the thigh of your supporting leg.

At the same time, push directly forward (not upward) with your rear foot. Of course as soon as you pull your lead leg out, you will begin to fall forward. The movement of your lead leg has to be fast, therefore, to make it back down to the floor to stop your fall.

At the completion of your move, your lead foot should be about 1.5 to 2 feet ahead of its starting position, and your rear foot should not have moved. Depending upon the tactical situation, you can now resume a normal balance by either sliding your rear foot forward to continue to attack or pursue your opponent, or you can push off your lead foot to move back out of range. For now, don't worry about making any strikes, just maintain your guard position and practice the footwork.

The key to this movement is to not shift your weight to the rear before you lift your lead foot. If you do this, you will not only lose speed, you will also telegraph your intentions to your opponent and give him additional reaction time to avoid or counter your strike. You can tell if you are shifting your weight back by assuming your guard stance and having your training partner hold his palm a fraction of an inch behind your back. If you shift your weight, you'll touch his palm.

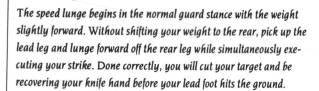

The speed lunge begins in the normal guard stance with the weight slightly forward. Without shifting your weight to the rear, pick up the lead leg and lunge forward off the rear leg while simultaneously executing your strike. Done correctly, you will cut your target and be recovering your knife hand before your lead foot hits the ground.

Another symptom of shifting your weight prior to lunging is that your body will be propelled upward by your rear leg rather than straight forward. The more weight on the rear leg at the time you push off, the higher you will go. To eliminate this, tie a string between two supports about a foot in front of your face. The height of the string should match your height when in a guard stance. Now practice the speed lunge. If you do it correctly, your head will pass under the string. If you push upward rather than forward, you'll hit it.

Incorporating Strikes into the Lunge

Once you begin to feel comfortable with this footwork, you can learn to incorporate strikes into it. Start with a downward vertical cut, aiming for your imaginary opponent's knife hand or forearm (or, if he keeps his knife to the rear, his lead hand). Without any preliminary tensing, do a

speed lunge and simultaneously execute a short downward cut with your knife. Your blade hand should leave the guard position, extend in a short vertical arc, and immediately recover to the guard position. This entire movement, if performed correctly, should be completed before your lead foot comes back to rest on the floor. At the very least, you must make contact with your target before your lead foot touches. If you had the footwork down well before practicing the strike, this will come quickly, and you'll be amazed at how fast you'll be hitting.

This move takes a long time to master, but it is well worth the effort. This one move, done

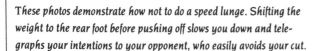

These photos demonstrate how not to do a speed lunge. Shifting the weight to the rear foot before pushing off slows you down and telegraphs your intentions to your opponent, who easily avoids your cut.

correctly, could end a knife fight before your opponent has a chance to try to cut you. Not only could you draw first blood and possibly inflict a debilitating wound, the psychological effect of scoring with a lighting-fast cut during the initial seconds of a fight could convince your opponent that he is totally outclassed.

DEFENSIVE FOOTWORK

The next type of footwork I will discuss is defensive or evasive footwork. The purpose of this type of movement is to get you out of the path of your opponent's blade. In some cases, it will leave you within range to execute a counterstrike, while in others it will take you completely out of cutting range.

There are two basic types of defensive footwork: linear and lateral.

Linear Footwork

Linear defensive footwork consists simply

of backing up away from your opponent's strike. By using the sliding boxing-style footwork described earlier, you can quickly back away from an attack while maintaining balance and control. If you angle your body by leaning backward from the waist or tucking your midsection in, you can make this footwork even more effective. With your knife held in your lead hand, you also have sufficient reach, even while moving backward, to cut your opponent's extended knife hand.

Alternately, you can step straight backward with your lead foot, reversing your stance to avoid an incoming strike. This puts you at a momentary disadvantage because your knife hand is in the rear but can be effective in certain circumstances.

Linear defensive footwork is limited because it is predictable and requires a clear area to your rear to be effective. If your opponent realizes that you have a habit of moving straight back, he may decide to rush you. There is no way you will be able to move backward for any great distance at the same rate he can move forward. Also, unless you're in a perfectly level, open area, you'll soon run into or trip over something.

Lateral Footwork

Lateral footwork takes you out of the path of your opponent's strikes by moving sideways or

This gives you a momentary advantage to get in your own strikes.

Finally, after you have completed your strikes, it is much easier and safer to break contact to resume your guard stance from a position beside your opponent. Breaking contact directly in front of your opponent leaves you vulnerable to being cut as you withdraw.

The theoretical model for lateral footwork is a triangle. If you are in your guard stance, the spot directly between your feet (below your center of gravity) can be imagined to be one corner of a triangle. If your opponent attacked with a straight thrust at your chest, you could avoid it by taking a diagonal step forward with your right foot (and twisting your body parallel to the line of his thrust). The position of your

Forward lateral movement using the triangle principle is demonstrated here. Note how it not only takes the defender out of the path of the incoming stab, but puts him in range for an immediate counter to the armpit and even adds power to the thrust.

diagonally. This has several advantages.

First, it uses less space and is therefore perfect for enclosed or cluttered areas where attacks often occur. By moving laterally, you can also position yourself in an area where your opponent is unable to strike you, yet you are within range for your own cut or thrust.

Lateral movement can also disorient your opponent and force him to change his focus.

right foot is now a second corner of the triangle. Had you stepped diagonally forward with your left foot instead, you would have created the third corner.

If instead of moving forward, you chose to avoid the thrust by taking a diagonal step to your left rear with your left foot, you would have created the second corner of a different triangle to your rear.

Here is an example of backward lateral movement. As the attacker slashes, our hero steps diagonally back out of the path of the stick and delivers a cut to the wrist. Note again how footwork adds power to the cut.

The concept of the triangle is just that, a concept. It is intended to keep you thinking of diagonal movement but not to restrict your movement. Don't draw triangles on the floor and try to follow them like the footprints in cheap dance lessons. Realize that every triangle you create with your movement will be a different size and shape, and every time you resume a balanced guard stance, you begin a new triangle. The concept is just there to remind you to move diagonally.

Diagonal movement is preferable to direct moves to either side because it complements the body angling that is needed to avoid your opponent's attacks successfully. It also leaves you close enough to your opponent to do some cutting of your own. When you make a cut or thrust in conjunction with a diagonal step, you'll increase its power substantially over the same strike made from a stationary position. Finally, diagonal movement allows you to maintain your guard stance more easily as you move, keeping your defenses tight.

As you read further and get into some of the example techniques shown in later chapters, pay close attention to the footwork shown in the photographs. Watch how the position of the feet changes from one photo to another and note what effect that movement has on each fighter's ability to continue the fight. A picture really is worth a thousand words (and a hell of a lot easier to include in a book!).

CHAPTER FIVE

Zones of Attack and Defense

To simplify the study of knife fighting, I have divided the areas of the body into five "zones." The use of these zones provides a convenient reference for strikes to different areas and forms the basis for my defensive knife-fighting system. It also makes practicing with a partner much easier. Instead of asking him to strike at a specific area of your body, you can just tell him the number of the zone in which that area is located.

The five zones can be visualized by a cross consisting of one vertical and one horizontal line having a dot at its intersection. The cross delineates four quadrants for angular attacks, and the dot at its center represents linear thrusting attacks.

The numbering system is *based on the perspective of the defender.* You can visualize it by standing in a fighting stance and imagining a cross in front of you. The upper left quadrant of the cross, which would include the left side of your upper body and head, is zone one. The upper right quadrant is zone two. The lower left quadrant is zone three, and the lower right is zone four. Any attacks coming straight toward your body's centerline are considered to be in zone five.

This photo shows the five defensive zones as they are defined in a stationary guard stance.

The zone system is not just intended to fill pages in this book (although it helps). In addition to providing a convenient reference system, it teaches two important points. The first point is that *your reactions to all attacks within a* your response should be the same as if he attempted a left-handed backhand thrust to the left side of your chest (also zone one). This same rule applies regardless of what weapon your opponent is wielding or if he has a weapon at all. By learning several basic responses to attacks in all five zones, you can deal with any attack coming from any angle without hesitation. This is different from many traditional martial arts and classical weapons systems where the response to a downward strike is different than that for an inward strike, which is also different from that for a backhand strike. By learning a few techniques well and applying them to many different attacks, you'll be a much better fighter than if you knew a thousand different techniques but couldn't do any of them well enough to use in a fight.

The second advantage of the zone system is

The elbow is the center of the zone cross hairs. The boundaries between zones are determined by natural body movement. Here a defensive hand cut is demonstrated at various levels in zone one. As the movement is executed at lower and lower levels, the hand naturally turns over, delineating the boundary at zones 1 and 3.

zone should be the same. What this means is that any attack that enters in zone one is handled using the same response. For example, if your opponent attempts a right-handed inward slash to the left side of your neck (zone one), that it promotes natural responses to attacks. The more natural a response, the easier, quicker, and more powerful it will be. The key to this is to imagine that the center of the cross identifying the five zones is located at the elbow of your knife-wielding arm. Whenever your arm moves, the cross moves with it. If your elbow moves right, the cross moves right. If you crouch down, the cross lowers.

Following this principle, any attack that enters from the area above and to the left of your elbow is in zone one and will receive a zone one response. Anything below and to your right of your elbow is in zone four, and so on.

The reason for this is simple. Remember that an attack at any angle in zone one receives the same response. Imagine that you are in a fighting stance and your opponent attacks with a right-handed, horizontal inward slash at your neck level. Your response is to slash the inside of his wrist before his knife reaches you, intercepting its motion. You'll notice that to do this, the most natural motion is to slash to your left with the point of your blade upward.

Now repeat this drill, but this time your opponent's strike will come at a slightly lower level. He will still be attempting a horizontal inward slash, and you will meet it by cutting the inside of his wrist. Without changing the level of your stance, continue the drill, each time having the attack thrown at a slightly lower level. You'll find that when the level of the attack reaches the horizontal level of your elbow, your movement becomes less comfortable. When it falls below the level of your elbow, your cut will not only feel very awkward, it will also no longer stop your opponent's

strike and will actually deflect it into your body.

Now have your partner throw another slash below the level of your elbow, but this time respond by executing your cut with the point of your knife facing downward, your palm facing forward. This will not only feel more natural, but will be a much more effective cut.

The point where you switched from a point-up cut to a point-down one is where you crossed the line from zone one to zone three. The zones defined themselves by your feeling which movements were natural and which were awkward.

If you conduct similar drills approaching the other imaginary boundaries between zones, you will experience the same thing. The only exception is the area of zone one very near its vertical boundary. It is more natural to intercept attacks in this area with your palm facing forward (point of your knife to the left), as you would in zone two. As such, the vertical boundary between zones one and two is not exactly vertical, but the basic concept still applies.

As you look at the photos in this book, and during your practice with a partner, bear in mind that the numbering of the zones is based on the perspective of the person *receiving* a cut or thrust. As such, if you execute a right-handed inward slash, even though your movement occurred in zone two, you attacked into your opponent's zone one, so that is considered a zone one strike.

CHAPTER SIX

Basic Cuts and Thrusts

To be effective as an offensive knife fighter, you must master the correct methods of slashing and thrusting. As you become proficient with these, you can integrate them into your practice of footwork and combine them with your defensive responses to complete your arsenal of knife-fighting skills.

The techniques described here are by no means the only cuts and thrusts you can deliver with a knife, but they form the basis for all such techniques. Remember the concept of five zones? When defending against attacks, the goal was to realize that any attack at any angle within a zone is basically the same and can be dealt with in the same way. This same principle of generality applies for offensive strikes. If you take a perfectly horizontal inward slash and deliver it at a slightly downward angle, it's not a new technique, just a variation on the same theme.

First, let's look at slashes and cuts. Note that I use these terms interchangeably. Some people don't consider them to be the same, but again, we're striving for simplicity and to grasp general principles that can be applied to a variety of situations. To some, a slash is a quick movement,

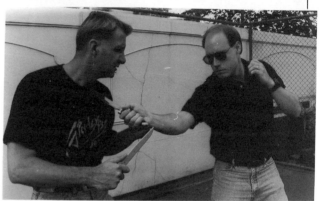

The inward slash. Note that this is a tight movement, not a wide swing, and that the full length of the knife edge is drawn through the target.

while a cut is more deliberate, slower, and more powerful. I don't make this distinction because the way you strike a particular target depends on the situation at that exact moment. If the target will only be exposed for a fraction of a second and your opponent can possibly cut you as you come in, a speedy movement to seize that momentary opportunity is in order. If, on the other hand, your opponent is already wounded or stunned and you have his knife hand positioned safely out of the way, you may have the luxury of being able to sacrifice speed for power to administer a coup de grace and finish the fight. The technique of the two movements is identical, but the emphasis in their delivery is tailored to the situation at hand. This is common sense, a good thing in knife fighting, so I needn't dwell upon it any further.

INWARD SLASH

The first cut I'll describe is the inward slash. Starting from a guard stance (and presumptuously assuming that you're right-handed), begin extending your knife arm toward a point

about 6 to 8 inches to the right (your right) of the intended target. Throughout most of this movement, the point of your knife will be upward and your palm facing to the left. As your knife arm nears full extension, turn your hand palm up and draw an arc from right to left through your target. Continue the fluid motion of the cut to withdraw your arm either directly back to your guard position or to a point near your left shoulder where you'll be cocked for a follow-up backhand strike.

As with all cuts, you want to make the base of the knife edge strike the target first and then draw the full length of the edge through the target to cut deeply. This is much more effective than hacking into a target. The knife edge is very much like a miniature saw. If examined microscopically, it can be seen to consist of many tiny teeth. To cut effectively, especially in flesh, these teeth must be drawn through the material being cut. It's just like cutting a steak. You don't hack away at it, you use the entire blade edge to slice the meat efficiently.

When executing an inward slash, don't extend your arm to the point where the elbow is locked,

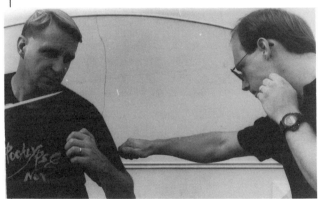 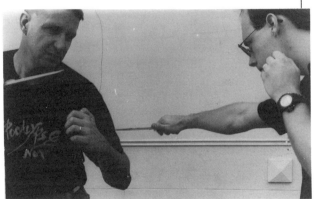

The backhand slash. The movement of the elbow and the arm should flow smoothly together, and as always, the knife edge should be drawn through the target.

as it can easily be broken in this position. Also, the bent elbow allows the arm to torque more efficiently, adding power to the cut. Another common mistake when executing this cut is to swing the arm wide. This leaves you open to being cut and slows the technique down considerably. Keep the movement tight and fast.

The inward slash can be directed offensively to practically any part of your opponent's body, but the favored targets are the face, neck, arm, and knee. Defensively, this is the movement used when executing cuts to your opponent's arm when he attacks in zone one.

The inward slash is not limited to a horizontal plane of motion. The same basic movement can be adjusted to strike at any height, at downward diagonal angles, or at upward diagonal angles. The movement remains unchanged; the angle is simply adjusted to take advantage of a particular opening or to hit a specific target. Taken to its logical extremes, this same motion, when executed at steep upward or downward diagonal angles, becomes a vertical upward or downward slash.

BACKHAND SLASH

The backhand slash is the next basic cutting technique. As its name indicates, it is performed with a backhand movement.

From your guard stance, lift your right elbow so that it is pointing straight at the intended target. Now extend your arm so the knife is lashed out in an arc. As the base of the blade strikes, follow through and draw the knife edge through the target. Then quickly withdraw your hand and recover to the guard position.

Continued practice of this technique will result in a blending of the movements of lifting the elbow and extending the arm into one fluid motion. This will telegraph the move less and make it harder for your opponent to defend against it.

The backhand slash, like the inward slash, can be delivered at any level and at a variety of upward or downward diagonal angles. Like the inward slash, it also has both offensive and defensive applications. For a right-hander, it is used most often to defend against attacks into zones two and four.

THRUST

Thrusting is the other major type of movement with the knife. In its simplest form, a thrust is any movement in which the point of the knife is used to puncture a target. However, just as the terms slashing and cutting can be used to reflect subtle differences in the way a cutting technique is executed, the terms thrusting and stabbing create images of slightly different actions. In general, a stab suggests a quick, darting movement that is not heavily committed. A thrust, on the contrary, indicates a sustained follow through of the technique and deep target penetration. Again, the technique and physical execution of the two may be identical, but the degree of power transmitted to the target will vary to take advantage of particular tactical opportunities. For the sake of simplicity, just remember that for our purposes, the terms are interchangeable.

Straight and Angular Thrusts

There are essentially two different types of thrusts: straight and angular. Straight thrusts are exactly that, thrusting attacks that are directed on a straight line toward the oppo-nent's body. Angular thrusts, however, are thrown on a variety of angles, either in linear motions or in short arcs. In many cases, angular thrusts resemble a boxer's hooks and upper-cuts and can be applied in much the same way.

Executing a straight thrust is much like throwing a boxer's jab. The only major difference is that the palm of the hand should face upward when the blade hits, rather than downward as in a jab. By keeping the palm upward, you maintain a straight, strong wrist angle that will absorb the impact of the blade's contact without damaging the hand or wrist. This position also ensures that your elbow stays slightly bent, even at full extension. This protects you from falling victim to an arm lock or elbow break. Finally, for attacks to the body, the palm-up position orients the plane of the blade horizontally, making it easier for it to slide between ribs.

The straight thrust can be delivered at a variety of levels and to numerous targets. Some of the best targets for this attack include the eyes, the neck and throat, the armpit, the chest and abdomen, the groin and thigh, and, from behind, the kidneys. For low-level attacks, it is best if the straight thrust is delivered with

The straight thrust. Note how the thumb guides the point of the blade accurately to the target. The palm should remain facing upward while the elbow stays down and slightly bent.

the knees bent to lower the entire body. This minimizes the exposure of your head and upper body as you hit low.

When thrown in tight, the straight thrust is similar to a boxer's uppercut, since the arm does not even approach full extension before it hits. This type of straight thrust works very well when combined with lateral footwork that places you outside your opponent's stance. Standing safely off to the side, you are in perfect position to pump a few short thrusts into his abdomen. These thrusts can be backed by a rotation of the hips and straightening of the legs. This same thrusting movement also works well when thrown at an upward angle through the diaphragm into the heart or under the chin into the mouth and possibly the brain.

The method of delivering angular thrusts is similar to that of throwing diagonal slashes. Like diagonal slashes, angular thrusts are delivered either inward or backhanded. The major difference in the movement is, of course, that the point of the knife, not the edge, is directed at the target.

To execute an inward angular thrust, start in the standard guard position. Let your knife hand drift a few inches to your right then extend your arm at a slightly inward angle toward your target. Your hand should be palm down, and your thumb should guide it toward the target. Performed correctly, it should feel as if you were reaching over a short wall to throw the technique, because your elbow will be up and your forearm basically parallel to the floor. The power for this thrust comes from a quick rotation to the left of your shoulders and hips, much like a boxer's hook.

When thrown at very low targets like the groin, the inward thrust changes slightly in that the elbow stays low and the point of the knife is directed diagonally upward into its target. The body mechanics that provide power for the thrust remain unchanged.

The best targets for inward angular thrusts are the same as for straight thrusts, but with this thrust, you can hit them from many more angles.

Backhand Thrusts

Backhand angular thrusts are similar to the straight thrust; however, they are begun to the left of your body and angled inward in a backhand motion. From the guard stance, let your knife hand drift several inches to the left so it is

These photos demonstrate an inward angular thrust. Again, the thumb guides the knife point for accurate placement.

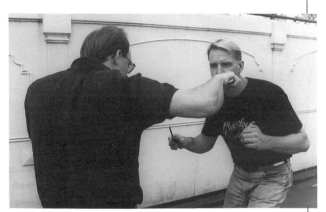

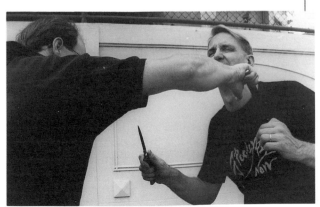

positioned near your left shoulder. Now turn it palm up, so your thumb and the point of your knife face toward your target. Then thrust your knife, guided by your thumb, in a straight line or slight arc toward the target. You can increase the power in this thrust by dropping your right shoulder slightly as you throw the technique and by stepping forward with your right leg at the same time. The targets for this thrust are the same as previously mentioned.

A powerful, well-executed thrust can bury the blade of your knife up to the hilt in your opponent's body. While this was of course the intent of the thrust to begin with, every success brings new problems. In this case, the problem is getting your knife back out to do some more damage and to protect you from having the same done to you, either by your opponent or one of his buddies.

The backhand angular thrust. The power for this strike comes from the triceps and shoulder muscles.

Withdrawal

Withdrawing your knife from a wound creates several problems. Aside from the writhing and screaming of the person on the other end, your knife will now be covered with blood, making the handle slippery and difficult to grasp. The blade of your knife can also be stuck in the target because of suction or muscular contraction and spasm in the wound area. If you happened to hit a bone, your blade point can be stuck into it. Likewise, if you hit a joint or hit between two bones, your blade can be lodged between them. Finally, if you went through clothing to hit your

target, you have to worry about the additional resistance of the clothing when removing your knife and keep from getting the guard of your knife (if any) tangled in it.

To overcome these problems, I have developed a standard method of knife withdrawal that combines two techniques: the push off and the comma cut.

A push off is simply the act of using your free hand to push your opponent away as you withdraw your blade. This accomplishes several things. First, the pushing force of your free hand makes withdrawing your knife from your opponent's body much easier since it stabilizes his body while you pull on the knife. Secondly, a hard push will unbalance your opponent and move him away from you quickly, making it difficult for him to land a cut of his own as you break contact.

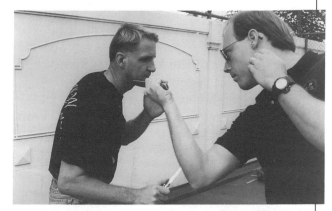

The comma cut gets its name because of the motion of the cut and the wounds it produces resemble a comma. Comma cuts are used to withdraw your knife from a stab wound. Regardless of which thrusting technique you used to create the wound, your hand should be either palm up or palm down as it grips the handle of the knife. To execute a comma cut, maintain a firm grasp on the handle and simply turn your hand over as you pull back to free your blade.

For example, if you executed a straight thrust or backhand thrust into your target, your hand will be palm up as it grips the handle of your knife. To withdraw it with a comma cut, grip the handle securely and simultaneously turn your hand counterclockwise to a palm-down position as you pull back. The power for this comes from your shoulder and back muscles.

If you are withdrawing your knife after a successful inward angular thrust, your hand will start in a palm-down position. As you pull, rotate your entire hand (and consequently the knife as well) clockwise to a palm-up position.

The comma cut movement accomplishes several things that contribute to easy blade withdrawal. The rotation of the hand places the arm in a more natural position to pull with maximum force. Turning the knife blade forces the edge of the blade to literally cut its way out of the wound channel. This breaks the suction of the flesh on the knife blade. It also enlarges the size of the wound channel tremendously, creating a devastating wound. Size, however, is not the only measure of the effectiveness of wounds created with this cut. The natural surface tension of the flesh and the contraction of underlying muscle tissue can often stem or greatly reduce the bleeding of a straight puncture wound. The arc-shaped wound created by a comma cut is self-supporting, meaning that the natural tension of the flesh cannot cause it to close. It will therefore bleed much more profusely than a straight puncture wound.

An additional benefit of the comma cut is that it often allows you to cut targets on withdrawal that you missed with your initial thrust. For example, if you thrusted at your opponent's carotid artery but miscalculated or your thrust was deflected, you may have still punctured his neck but missed the artery. A good comma cut will create a cutting arc within the flesh of the neck that will most likely sever the carotid, the jugular vein, and anything else in close proximity.

The movement of the comma cut also forms the basis of many of the counter cuts that can be used to cut your opponent after he has already blocked one of your initial strikes. These techniques will be explained later in the chapter on counterdefenses.

When you practice all your techniques that end with a thrust, include a comma cut with a simultaneous push off to simulate withdrawing your blade and breaking contact. These two techniques done simultaneously will make blade withdrawal quick and positive.

It should be noted that the only case in which a comma cut is not advisable is when your blade is thrust between your opponent's ribs. Turning the blade can actually cause it to become stuck between the rib bones, so a push off and a straight backward pull are recommended in this circumstance.

Although I'll talk about combinations of cuts and thrusts in later chapters, there is one combination that deserves special mention, so I'll describe it here. In the Filipino martial arts, it is called *abanico*, which comes from the Spanish word for fan. This technique is basically a combination of an inward slash and a backhand slash thrown in very quick succession. The movement is performed mostly by the wrist and resembles the motion that you would use to fan yourself, hence its name.

To perform an *abanico*, execute a normal inward slash at any angle toward an imaginary target. As your knife cuts through the target and just passes it, quickly rotate your wrist to turn your palm down and cut back through the target from the opposite direction with a backhand stroke. Your blade should not pass the target more than a couple of inches after the first cut before it reverses direction.

When you feel comfortable with this move, reverse the order of the cuts so you begin with a backhand strike and follow immediately with an inward cut. After this begins to flow for you, practice doing two *abanicos* in sequence. You'll quickly see that this technique relies entirely on wrist and forearm finesse and can be done *very* quickly.

Like all other cuts, the angles for the cuts that make up an *abanico* movement can vary from horizontal to vertical and every angle in between. If you chose to do an *abanico* against your opponent's exposed neck, it would be

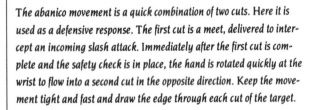

The abanico movement is a quick combination of two cuts. Here it is used as a defensive response. The first cut is a meet, delivered to intercept an incoming slash attack. Immediately after the first cut is complete and the safety check is in place, the hand is rotated quickly at the wrist to flow into a second cut in the opposite direction. Keep the movement tight and fast and draw the edge through each cut of the target.

executed on a horizontal angle, cutting the target on both sides. An *abanico* against your opponent's extended arm would be done vertically to cut the arm on both the top and bottom.

I'll explain later that I don't think that multiple cuts against an opponent are practical, but the *abanico*, because of its inherent speed, can allow you to cut your attacker twice in little more time than it takes for a single cut. As such, I consider it a viable technique and one well worth mastering.

These are all the basic cutting and thrusting techniques that can be done with a knife.

Although you may think there are more, if you examine other strikes closely, you'll find that they are simply variations of those shown here. This is true not only of strikes with the standard grip, but those done with a knife held in a reverse grip. The arm and body movement is exactly the same. Only the grip and the angles at which the techniques are thrown vary.

CHAPTER SEVEN

Defensive Responses

As I have emphasized in previous chapters, knife fighting is primarily an offensive proposition. It is never a good idea to take a passive role and try to block your opponent's incoming strikes while you wait for an opening to counter. This is a sure way to get cut and maybe even get killed.

The world, however, is a decidedly imperfect place, and at times you won't have the luxury of initiating your offense before your opponent does. You will have no choice but to defend yourself first before seizing the initiative and going on the offense.

In the chapter outlining the five zones used in knife fighting, I explained that the primary advantages of the zone system were that it teaches you unity of technique (using the same response for a variety of attacks in a particular zone) and that it promotes natural actions. By mastering a few natural responses and learning to apply them to a variety of attacks, it is possible to develop a simple, effective system of defense.

First let's consider what constitutes a good defensive action. If your opponent tries to cut you and you do something to avoid or prevent being cut, that can be considered an effective defensive action. That is also in keeping with the second basic rule of knife fighting. As you recall, the first rule of knife fighting is, *don't!* Well, the second rule is, if you can't avoid it and you have to get involved in a knife fight, *don't get cut!*

However, as I explained earlier, knife fighting is an offensive proposition. If any action that keeps you from getting cut is considered a good defensive action, then it follows that any action that damages your opponent while at the same time keeping you from getting cut is a better defensive action. That should be your goal.

MEETS, PASSES, AND FOLLOWS

In a knife fight, your knife hand becomes as important as any of your vital organs in keeping you alive. The same is true of your opponent. If you can render his knife (or weapon) hand useless, you have made him much less dangerous to you. In the Filipino martial arts, they use the analogy that taking away an opponent's weapon

(or weapon hand) is like taking the fangs from a snake. Although it may still look deadly, it is actually rendered harmless. Based on this principle, the third basic rule of knife fighting is to cut your opponent's attacking hand.

When applying this rule in a fight, there are three basic physical possibilities. The first is that you cut the opponent's hand and remain positioned in the path of his blade. This is called a meet. In the second, you move out of the path of the strike, cut your opponent's hand, and allow it to continue. This is referred to as a pass. The third possibility is that you move out of the path of your opponent's strike, allow it to continue and cut it after it passes. This is called a follow. These three techniques compose what I call defensive responses and are the foundation of my system of knife defense.

Meet

Let's look at a some specific examples that will help explain each of these techniques. You are in a guard stance (knife in your right hand)

A meet is a defensive response that intercepts your opponent's strike with a cut and leaves you still in its path. It is always followed by a safety check with the free hand to keep the opponent's strike from following through.

and facing an opponent who attacks with an inward right-handed slash toward your neck. This would fall into your zone one. If you respond by holding your ground and executing a cut targeted directly at your opponent's knife wrist, you are in essence "meeting" it head on, hence the term "meet." The advantage of this tactic is that it doubles the force of your cut by opposing the momentum of the attacker's hand, much like a head-on collision. The disadvantage is that it leaves you positioned "inside," between your opponent's arms and still in the path of his strike. This requires that you use your free hand as a "safety check" to control your opponent's knife hand after you cut it. It also leaves you vulnerable to being hit by his free hand.

Pass

Next your opponent attempts the same attack into your zone one. This time, though, you step back slightly and angle your upper body away from your opponent to remove yourself from the path of his strike. As his knife hand passes in front of you, you cut the inside

of his wrist and allow his hand to continue its arc. Since you do not stop the movement of his hand but allow it to pass by as you cut it, this is called a "pass." This technique allows you to cut your opponent's hand with almost as much force as a meet, but doesn't expose you to the danger of being cut as his strike follows through. In this particular example, it also allows you to move in behind your opponent's hand after it passes. In this position, it's quite easy for you to control and monitor him. Your opponent will also find it practically impossible to react defensively to any strikes you might throw from that angle.

Follow

The final defensive response is the "follow." Again using the same attack scenario, you step back slightly and angle your upper body away from your opponent as when doing a pass. However, instead of cutting the inside of his wrist as it passes, you let it pass and execute a backhand cut to the back of his knife hand. Your cut "follows" his knife hand to cut it. Because the angle of your cut does

A pass intercepts an attacker's strike with a cut but lets its motion continue as you move out of the path of the strike.

A follow gets you out of the way of an attacker's strike but leaves you in range to cut his hand after it goes by. This cut is not as powerful as a meet or a pass.

not meet your opponent's hand head on, this cut is considerably weaker than the previous two techniques. The advantage of the follow, however, is that your body weight and momentum are already committed forward as you execute your cut. By continuing that momentum, you can close with your opponent quickly and attack his exposed targets. The follow is also a useful defense against attacks with long, heavy weapons that develop a lot of momentum.

The three defensive responses work equally well for zones one through four and, with a little modification, zone five as well. By learning to apply these three responses to all five zones, you have a complete defensive system consisting of only 15 movements: efficiency through simplicity.

CHAPTER EIGHT

Defensive Strategies, Counters, and the Safety Check

Understanding the defensive responses and practicing them from a static position is not enough to make them effective in a real knife fight. You must learn to integrate them with footwork and other defensive tactics to be able to use them in a spontaneous combat situation. You must then learn to follow them up with cuts and thrusts of your own, combining offensive and defensive techniques into a total knife-fighting system.

FOOTWORK

I have already discussed the concept of defensive footwork in the chapter on footwork. As you practice the defensive responses, you will see how this concept is applied in defending and countering an opponent's attacks. As with the concept of zones, where your natural movement patterns delineated the boundaries of each area, let your natural responses serve as the basis of your defensive footwork. Each time you practice a defensive response, note how your foot position changes throughout the movement.

The advantage of the zone system when combined with the defensive responses is that it allows you to use uniform responses against any attacks within a particular zone. Here the same response works equally well against a right-handed inward slash or a left-handed backhand attack with a club.

This defensive movement shows how angling, footwork, body position-ing, and defensive responses can be combined. When the attacker throws a backhanded slash, the defender steps diagonally forward and angles away from the cut to the attacker's outside. He then delivers a meet to the attacker's knife arm, followed by a safety check, which controls the arm at the elbow. He then continues his movement to the attacker's outside, where he is safe from any subsequent attacks and in perfect position to deliver a follow-up thrust to the throat.

You will find that you are almost instinctively employing the linear and triangular defensive movements described in the footwork chapter. When performing a meet, you will most often be using triangular footwork, stepping diagonally forward to either evade or jam (move into) an attack. During a pass you will find yourself doing a slight linear movement to the rear or stepping diagonally backward. A follow will require a rearward linear movement followed by an immediate forward linear or diagonal movement. This may sound complicated, but it will come very naturally as you practice. Just let your feet take you where you need to go to accomplish the task at hand. As you become more proficient, your footwork will become more deliberate yet still retain its natural, instinctive responsiveness and speed.

ANGLING

An aspect of knife fighting that is closely related to footwork is angling. The concept of angling includes two basic tactics that allow you to avoid being cut while simultaneously putting you in a perfect position to cut your opponent. The first tactic is simply inclining (leaning) your upper body out of the path of your opponent's strike. When used alone, it allows you to evade an incoming strike without yielding ground to your opponent. This not only leaves you within range to do some cutting of your own, it gives you the capability to evade strikes when your mobility is restricted by surrounding obstacles. In many cases, such as when executing meets and passes, it also gives additional power to your cut by increasing the body torque behind the move. I have already described several examples of this tactic in the chapter on footwork. Additional examples appear in the technique section of this book.

The second aspect of angling deals with the physical positioning of your body with relation to your opponent. Essentially, this means putting your body where your opponent can't hurt you. I discussed this briefly in my description of the defensive responses. Basically, every attack thrown by your opponent has three distinct phases. For ease of reference, we'll call them the initial, middle, and final stages.

The initial stage is the portion of your opponent's movement that occurs just as the movement starts. In a knife strike, it would be just as your opponent's knife arm begins to extend, but before it gains enough momentum to strike with appreciable power. The middle stage is the middle portion of your opponent's movement. In this stage, momentum has already been built, and any contact would result in a significant transfer of force to the target. This is the stage during which your opponent wants to hit his target to get maximum force into his cut or thrust.

The final stage of a movement is the stage where the power of the strike has already been expended, but the arm continues on to full extension. This stage is normally only reached if a strike misses its target completely or the range to the target was underestimated or changed during the course of the strike.

If you imagine a backhanded horizontal slashing attack, the initial stage of the movement would correspond to the initial uncoiling of the cocked arm. As the arm nears full extension, it would enter the middle stage. This segment of the movement, in the center of the cutting arc, is the area where the strike has the most power. As the arm continues past full extension and past the intended point of contact with the target, its force dissipates rapidly. This is the final stage.

Defensive movements are safest when employed during the initial or final stages of an opponent's attack, either before or after his attack reaches full power. If you block or deflect his attack during these phases, he will be unable to apply enough force to do damage to you. Even if you are unable to execute an effective block, by simply positioning yourself in the initial or final stages of the arc of his attack, you will greatly minimize your chances of being seriously hurt by his strike.

When you block during the initial stage of a strike or apply pressure to prevent your opponent from extending his strike, it is called *jamming*. The best example of this would be applying pressure to the back of your attacker's elbow when he is preparing to throw a backhanded strike. This is most effective when combined with diagonal footwork that moves you forward into the line of the attack.

If your opponent throws a backhand strike and you move ahead of and in the same direction as the strike to position yourself in the final stage of its arc, you are moving to your opponent's outside. His outside is the area to either side of your opponent at the extreme range of a backhand strike. This is in contrast to your opponent's inside, which is basically the physical space in front of your opponent and between his outstretched arms. In general, angling to the outside is much safer than, and therefore preferable to, moving to the inside. This not only places you in a position where the power of your opponent's strike is minimal, it also protects you from his free hand, which would have to reach over or under his knife arm to get to you.

PERCEPTION SPEED

To defend yourself properly against your opponent's attacks, you must be able to recognize them in time to react. The time it takes to do this is called your perception speed. Perception speed is developed only through practice. Drilling individual techniques and practicing knife sparring will develop your awareness and sensitivity to your opponent's movements that will allow you to react in a timely manner. You may be able to execute a technique with perfect form and power, but if you can't react quickly enough to execute the technique in a timely fashion, it won't do you any good.

Focus on Opponent's Key Body Parts

One way to hasten the development of your perception speed is to maintain proper eye focus. By learning to focus on certain key portions of your opponent's body, you will be able to identify his attacks in their earliest stages of initiation. The key parts of your opponent's body you need to focus on are those that move first in the execution of an attack: the shoulders, elbows, feet, and eyes.

Since we are concerned with an attacker using hand-held weapons, we know that he must use his hand and arm to maneuver these weapons. Even a mediocre opponent can be capable of making very quick strikes, therefore focusing on the weapon hand alone will not give you an edge in reacting to his attacks.

However, if you pay close attention to your training partner or watch yourself in a mirror as you practice your strikes, you'll see that before your knife hand can move, your shoulders move. The movement may not be great, but it is certainly perceptible. The reason is that any quick, powerful arm movement like a slashing or stabbing attack is initiated by the shoulder muscles. These muscles contract first to begin the arm's motion, then the muscles of the arm contract to continue the movement's momentum and give it a whip-like force. With practice, you can recognize the tensing or movement of your opponent's shoulders that precedes his attack. This gives you a few fractions of a second to begin to react before his weapon hand is in motion. This edge in timing is all you need to make sure your defensive action is there when you need it.

Watch for Opponent's Telegraphing

The preliminary motion before initiating a strike is called telegraphing. Good fighters practice to eliminate any movements that might telegraph their blows to their opponent. Most also keep their arms and shoulders in constant motion when fighting to cover any preliminary movements. This makes identifying preliminary shoulder movement more difficult, but not impossible. To help you identify attacks in their early stages, you should also focus on your opponent's elbows. The elbow is located halfway between the shoulder and the hand. As such, it must move slightly before the hand can move. Because of its location, it must also move at half the speed of the hand. It is therefore much easier to follow. By watching your opponent's elbows as well as his shoulders, you can be aware of his attacks in their early stages and have a little extra time to mount an effective defense.

Another body part that often telegraphs an opponent's intentions is the feet. Most of the time, it will be necessary to take a step to get within cutting range. If this step comes before the strike, it can give you advance warning to take defensive action. Some unskilled opponents will shift their weight to their rear leg before springing off it to execute a lunging attack. This weight shift can also be detected by watching your opponent's feet. When you see it, attack! At that moment, your opponent will be thinking about his offensive move and will be ill-prepared to defend himself.

Some fighters telegraph their intentions by focusing their gaze on their intended targets immediately before they strike. By being aware of where your opponent is focusing his eyes, you can often detect his intent to attack before he launches his strike and be ready and waiting to cut him.

Use Your Peripheral Vision

After reading all this, you're probably wondering how you can focus on all these parts of your opponent's body at once. The answer is to use your peripheral vision. The center of your focus should be on your opponent's upper chest. This will allow you to concentrate most closely on the movements of his shoulders and elbows. However, it will not prevent you from seeing the rest of his body, including his eyes and feet, in your peripheral vision. Although peripheral vision is not as acute as the vision in the center of your gaze, it is very effective in picking up movement, which is exactly what you want to do.

It should be noted that in detecting movement, you are not only concerned with those actions that signal an imminent attack with the weapon hand. As I've said before, knife fighting is a total body endeavor. That's true for both you and your opponent. There are no rules prohibiting him from kicking you in the groin or punching you in the face before he cuts you, so be aware of this possibility and be ready to react to other attacks too. When you react to other attacks, it should also be with the idea of a total body commitment. Don't become fixated on using your knife to defend against every attack. You may cut an attacker's leg and prevent him from kicking you, but in doing so you may lower your guard and give him a variety of open targets above your waist. Remember, your knife is a complement to your existing body weapons, not a replacement for them.

Avoid Telegraphing Your Intentions

Focusing your gaze on a specific area of your opponent's body also helps you avoid showing

fear by nervous eye movements or by getting into a "stare-down" with him. By having a steady focus, you exude confidence and have a very businesslike appearance. You will not be affected by his stare and can focus your gaze calmly on him. This can have tremendous psychological effect in an encounter, since a man who appears undaunted when entering into a life or death situation can't help but strike fear into the heart of his opponent.

You've probably realized that the same subtle movements that telegraph your opponent's actions can also give your intentions away to him. You must therefore practice to eliminate or at least minimize your telegraphing. You can do this by practicing solo in front of a mirror and watching for signs of telegraphing and by getting feedback from your practice partners. You can also avoid telegraphing with your eyes by practicing cutting targets using only your peripheral vision. Keep your vision focused as you would on your opponent's chest and practice cutting other areas of his body without shifting your gaze. This can be done with life-size practice targets made of cardboard or by using a rubber training knife with a partner.

With all this said, you must still remember that a knife in anyone's hand is an extremely deadly weapon. Although you should never fix your focus onto it exclusively, you must always be aware of where it is. If you lose track of your opponent's blade, when you find it again it may be sticking out of you!

Presenting the Least Vulnerable Targets

This brings me to another basic rule of knife fighting: *If you can't avoid getting cut, get cut in a place that is the least vulnerable to serious damage from a knife wound.* Although this may sound obvious, it is not as simple as it might seem. If you realize that there's a blade on its way toward you and you're not prepared to defend against it in the preferred manner (i.e., chopping off the hand holding it, then following with a finishing strike), at least try to protect your vital targets from being cut. It will still be unpleasant, but a cut to the outside of your forearm is preferable to one to the neck. We'll look at other last-ditch techniques later when we talk about ambushes and buying time to draw your blade.

We've already established that one of the most important defensive principles in knife fighting is to cut your opponent's attacking hand. By following this principle, you turn every one of his attacks into one of yours and maximize your chances of disarming him. However, just because you cut his knife arm as he's attacking doesn't mean you've rendered his attack harmless. Unless you are using a large, heavy-bladed knife, the momentum of your cut will probably not be enough to stop his attack completely. His arm will likely continue its motion after he's been cut, and he may still be capable of cutting you. To protect against this, every defensive cut should be combined with or immediately followed by a safety check with the free hand.

SAFETY CHECK

A safety check is simply a block, parry, or check executed with the free hand to control your opponent's knife hand and keep it from cutting you. It is also used to hold his hand in place for a fraction of a second while you execute a counter. When performing a meet or follow, your safety check will follow the same line as your knife hand, trailing several inches behind it. During a pass, it opposes the movement of your knife hand, guiding your opponent's hand into your blade, then past it.

In some cases, you will not have a chance to cut your opponent's weapon hand before you have to stop it. If this happens, you can use a safety check as a block or parry against the wrist or forearm of your attacker's weapon arm. These blocks and parries can be done with the palm of your free hand or the outside of your forearm, but whatever surface you use, make them quick and powerful. Long, sustained pushes are not recommended since your attacker can simply pull his hand back to cut your blocking arm, as we'll learn a bit later.

When it is necessary to control an attacker's knife hand so you can follow with more than one counterstrike, safety checks will usually become grabs. You will simply grasp your opponent's knife wrist to prevent his arm from moving while you carve on him with your other hand. While this may seem to be a safe tactic,

giving you even greater control of his knife hand, it actually leaves you open to getting your wrist or hand badly cut. By twisting or rolling his hand, your opponent can easily position the edge of his blade against your wrist and cut you. Your natural reaction when this happens, unfortunately, is to hang on tight, guaranteeing that you'll be cut.

To avoid this, when you grab his wrist, position your hand as close to his as possible rather than grasping close to his forearm. This limits his wrist mobility and makes it harder to maneuver his blade to cut you. By pulling or pushing his arm after you grab, you also make it difficult for him to position his hand for a cut. If you feel his hand turning and think you're about to be cut, throw his hand away from you immediately. You may still get cut, but not as badly as if you left your hand anchored to his wrist while he was cutting. I will discuss techniques for dealing with wrist grabs later in the chapter on counterdefenses.

While we're on the subject of grabbing, you should note that grabbing your opponent's clothing to control, maneuver, or unbalance him is also a viable tactic and one that is popular among street fighters and knife fighters who've refined their skills in prison. It is usually much easier to control an opponent's arm by getting a good grip on his sleeve instead of his wrist. Grabbing his lapel or collar and pulling him off balance into a thrust is also a good tactic. This tactic is so good, in fact, that you should practice defending against it in your sparring sessions, since you stand a good chance of encountering it during a fight. The best defense against this move, of course, is not to be grabbed in the first place. Evasive footwork and cutting your attacker's free hand as he tries to grab you will accomplish this. If he does get hold of you, cover your midsection with your free arm, step backward quickly, and stab to his ribs, neck, or face. This will keep him from closing on you. If he doesn't automatically let go, slash the inner elbow of his grabbing hand or stab the spot between his biceps and triceps muscles. Don't try carving on his wrist or fingers because you are likely to cut yourself with your own blade in the scuffle.

Once you've mastered all the defensive

skills described thus far, you'll be able to recognize an attack in its early stages and react quickly with an effective defensive cut, backed by a safety check. If you're lucky, the cut you make to your attacker's knife hand will prompt him to drop his knife and put an end to the fight. If you're even luckier, you will be carrying a big enough knife to sever his hand completely (the ultimate disarm) and guarantee an end to the fight. Unfortunately, reality dictates that this will not always be the case, and at least one, if not more, follow-up cuts or thrusts will be necessary.

COUNTERSTRIKES

If you witness the exponents of some schools of knife fighting during practice, you will notice that, after an initial defensive cut, they will follow up with 10 or more counter cuts and thrusts. During this flurry of counterstrikes, the defender's practice partner stands obediently in place, knife arm still extended, as he is methodically reduced to stew meat. While I agree with the concept of practicing to take a fight to its logical ultimate conclusion, the death of your opponent, I don't agree that this is the way to do it.

We've established that a person has to be either stupid or crazy to want to start a knife fight. Crime statistics prove, however, that there is an abundance of people roaming our streets who are gifted with just such stupidity. Although these miscreants may well be foolish enough to provoke a blade-to-blade contest, I can't believe that *anyone* would be stupid enough to stand there and continue to be cut after their initial move is stopped. Once a person realizes he's being cut, he will instinctively do something to try to stop that from happening again. At the very least, he'll withdraw his arm and try to protect himself from further cuts. If he can maintain his presence of mind, he may continue to fight (often much harder than before he was cut) or break contact altogether and run. He will *not* freeze in place to allow you to do a Benihana routine on him.

I know that some books have described knife fights in which people stood toe-to-toe and slashed away at one another for minutes on end. I don't dispute the fact that such things have happened, I'm just saying that you, the reader of this book, are intelligent enough not to get into such situations. Both participants in such instances had to be insane to continue to stand there and cut on each other. You would have either had the sense not to enter into such an altercation or the skill to bring an end to it quickly.

The point of the matter is, in a knife fight, once you cut someone, he will not stand still for long, thus making it difficult for you to cut him again. Based on this fact, it is reasonable to assume that, after your initial defensive cut, you will only be able to follow with one counterstrike. If both of your strikes connect well and if you're fast, you might be able to get in a second counterstrike, but two cuts is the anticipated norm. Borrowing a term from combat-shooting parlance, I refer to the practice of executing a defensive cut and following it with a counter as a double tap.

Double Tap

According to the double-tap concept, during every clash, you will try to strike your opponent twice. The first cut is targeted at what I refer to as a minor target. This is basically any target that, when cut, will have a telling effect but not bring about a quick death. In most cases, this target is your opponent's knife hand or arm. The second cut or thrust of the double tap is geared to a major target, or any target that, cut or punctured well, will take your opponent out of the fight either by causing disabling injury or inflicting a mortal wound.

The practice of double tapping applies equally well to both defensive and offensive actions. Defensively, the first cut will be one of the defensive responses (meet, pass, or follow). This will of course be followed by a safety check to control the opponent's knife hand or position it safely out of the way to create an opening for the second cut or thrust to a vital target. Offensively, the double tap minimizes your risk of being cut as you attack. Rather than attempting to hit a vital target with your first shot, using an initial cut to a minor target will bridge the gap and create an opening for a disabling or killing blow. Again, the use of the knife should be integrated into your total body arsenal. In double tapping, this means that the opening move does not necessarily have to be a cut with your knife. Kicks, punches, finger jabs, or practically any other type of initial hit can be used to set up your second cut or thrust. Moves of this type can often be even more effective than an opening cut since they take your opponent by surprise. When he sees you armed with a knife, he'll most likely expect you to make your first move with it. While he's busy watching your knife hand and waiting for it to come, you can catch him with a fist or a foot before following with your blade.

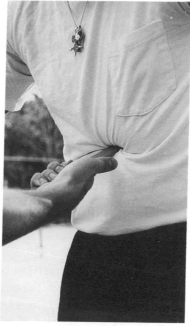 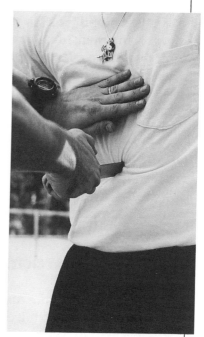

The specific targets attacked during a double tap depend upon the situation, your opponent's position, your position, and whether you are acting offensively or defensively. In general, however, the first cut must set up the second cut so it can be delivered very quickly, minimizing the time between strikes. To do this, the two strikes must flow together. After the first cut lands, the hand should automatically be positioned for the next strike.

The finishing hand position after the first strike in many ways will dictate the possible major targets for the second one. For example, if you are attacked with a low-level inward slash (zone three), your first cut could be a meet, cutting your opponent's wrist with your blade point down. This is followed immediately by a safety check with your free hand. The follow-through from your first cut should have left your knife hand positioned somewhere up near your left shoulder. In this position, it is cocked for an immediate backhand slash or thrust. Since your checking hand is keeping your opponent's weapon hand safely

Withdrawing your knife after a successful thrust can be a chore. The proper withdrawal technique, known as a comma cut, makes it much easier and safer. The comma cut combines a hard push off with the free hand and a simultaneous pulling and rotating of the knife hand. This not only frees the knife blade but greatly enlarges the wound channel.

out of the way down low, his upper body is exposed on that side. As such, your best move is to target your second strike to an exposed major target of his upper body, such as the eye or the neck. The follow through from that strike should then leave your hand cocked to deliver another cut or thrust if necessary. Like a good billiards player, you should use each hit to set you up for the next. Similarly, each of your hits should take advantage of your opponent's reaction to the previous one. For example, if you are able to slip in a quick stab to your opponent's groin, his natural reaction will be to double over. As his head is moving forward and down, the area under his chin will be exposed. A natural follow-up would be an upward thrust to that target. It will not only be exposed and easy to hit, it will be moving in the opposite direction of your blade, thereby doubling the force of your thrust.

Although, in general the two-hit rule stands, there is one exception to this rule that will allow you to get in an extra cut or sometimes even two during a brief clash. This exception is the *abanico* combination cut described in the chapter on basic cuts and thrusts. The speed of this technique can allow you to use it as if it were only a single cut.

A well-executed double tap should result in your blade cutting deeply or getting stuck deeply into some vital part of your opponent's anatomy. While this will be highly unpleasant for him, it will not necessarily prevent him from continuing his efforts to carve on you, either while you're still in close or as you withdraw and break away. To protect yourself from this, you need to learn to break contact safely. This is done by using a combination of a push off and, if recovering from a thrust, a comma cut. Refer to the chapter on basic cuts and thrusts for a detailed description of these techniques.

I have already emphasized that you should always practice and be prepared to take the fight to the very end: the death of your opponent. If, based on the situation, you decide to stop the fight short and vacate the area after wounding your attacker, it's your call. If you

decide up front that you're going to have to kill your attacker, once you've wounded him, continue cutting him for as long as you safely can to finish him off. If your first few cuts found their mark and you back off, you will have to close with him again if you decide to finish the job. If he's pumping blood all over the place, you could hang around and wait for him to bleed to death, but that's both inconvenient and uncertain. Moving in to finish the job with the knife exposes you to greater danger, especially if he's still armed.

If your opponent is already down, an easier and safer solution is to stay at a distance and stun him with a few well-placed kicks to the head. When the kicks have him sufficiently dazed, you can safely move in and finish with the knife. If your attacker is still on his feet, a solid kick to the knee will put him down. Then you can follow with the same drill.

It is curious to note that, in addition to the obvious danger of suffering bodily injury when confronting someone with a knife, these days there is a whole new danger to worry about: AIDS. As we all know, AIDS can be transmitted by mixing blood with an infected person. In a knife fight, you are desperately trying to slice up your opponent to take him out of the fight. In the process, it is also very likely that you will be cut. With blood flowing all over the place, the risk is obvious. Of course, if your life is on the line and the only choice you have is to defend it with a sharp blade, the threat of disease will be overshadowed by your immediate struggle for survival.

While on the subject of safety, you'll notice that in performing most techniques, your free hand closely follows your knife hand when making safety checks. In the heat of a fight, it is very possible that you could cut your own free hand during a quick exchange. To prevent this, practice your techniques slowly and gradually build speed after you've developed a sufficient degree of coordination. Finally, practice your moves with a sharp blade to develop the confidence to wield it quickly and skillfully.

CHAPTER NINE

Targets

A cut anywhere on your opponent's body is a victory for you in a knife fight. It will not only have a psychological effect on your opponent, in many cases even relatively shallow cuts to nonvital areas will induce physiological shock. However, cuts and thrusts to certain specific targets can have a much more telling effect than those delivered to other places. By learning which portions of human anatomy are most vulnerable to knife attacks, you can take full advantage of every opportunity you have to cut your opponent and bring an end to the fight quickly.

There are basically three types of targets that can be attacked with a knife. They are categorized by the type of damage they would suffer when cut or punctured.

DISABLING TARGETS

Disabling targets are targets that consist of key portions of the physical structure of the body. When these targets are cut or punctured, the function of that portion of the body is seriously impaired or rendered completely nonfunctional. Typical disabling targets include tendons, muscles, and nerve bundles located in the arms and legs. Tendons are the tissues that connect muscles to bones, transmitting the force of the contracting muscles to the bone and causing that limb to move. If these are cut, the muscle is disconnected from the bone, and that limb is effectively paralyzed.

Attacking the muscles that move the limbs directly is another way of impairing or disabling their action. The thickness of muscles makes them more difficult to cut completely than tendons, but a good solid cut can still paralyze your opponent's arm or leg.

Nerves carry messages from the brain to the muscles, controlling their actions. They also relay sensory input back to the brain. Nerves run through the body like electrical wires, entering the limbs in bundles and spreading out in a network. By attacking nerve bundles, you can not only induce tremendous pain, you can "short circuit" the nerve network for that limb, sending it into violent spasms and making coordinated movement impossible. The spinal cord is the main nerve bundle that runs from the brain down the spine, branching off to all parts of the body. If it is attacked directly near its source, the brain can be literally disconnected from the rest of the body, resulting in instantaneous death.

BLOOD VESSELS

Blood vessels compose the second category of knife target. The body contains an intricate network of blood vessels that circulate blood to all its tissues. Veins carry blood from the tissues back to the heart. The heart pumps the blood through the lungs to oxygenate it and then pumps it throughout the body via arteries. Whenever a blood vessel is cut and the body loses blood, the body tissues begin to be deprived of oxygen. As the volume of blood in the body decreases, the transfer of oxygen to the tissues of the body, especially the brain, becomes less and less efficient. Finally, the brain shuts down, and unconsciousness occurs. If the bleeding is

allowed to continue unchecked, brain damage and ultimately death result.

Since arteries carry blood away from the heart, the blood pressure in them is much higher than in veins. Consequently, they bleed much more profusely when cut. In fact, you had better beware when you land a solid slash that severs an artery, as you could literally be showered in blood. The fact that arteries carry oxygenated blood also makes them preferred targets over veins, since inducing the loss of oxygenated blood is your primary objective.

LIFE-SUPPORT ORGANS

The third type of target that is vulnerable to attack with a knife includes the body's life-support organs. These organs perform various functions that are necessary to keep a person alive. If they are damaged or destroyed, their ability to function is seriously degraded and death can occur. Some of these organs process the blood as it is circulated throughout the body and therefore also qualify as bleeding targets. These include the kidneys, the liver, and the spleen. The lungs are of course responsible for taking in oxygen and transmitting it to the blood. If punctured, their function will be seriously impaired, and oxygen deprivation results. The heart and brain are so integral to the function of the body that the results of a direct knife attack to these targets need not be described to be appreciated.

Now let's take a look at specific targets, their locations on the body, and how best to attack them. The easiest way to do this is to start with the front of the body and work from the top down. Then we'll look at the back of the body the same way.

FRONT TARGETS

The targets on the front of the body that are well suited to a knife attack are as follows:
• *Forehead.* The forehead is full of blood vessels and will bleed profusely when cut. A cut here will not cause serious injury, but it will cause blood to run down into your opponent's eyes, obscuring his vision and leaving him vulnerable to further attacks.

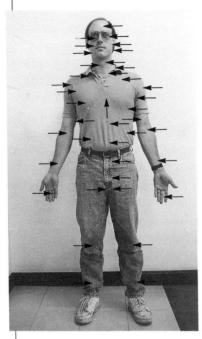

This photo shows the locations of the various targets on the front of the body that are well suited to being attacked with a knife.

• *Eyes.* Without vision, your opponent cannot fight. A direct attack to the eye will easily damage it and probably cause permanent blindness. Such an attack will also prompt an instinctive reaction to cover the eyes with both hands to protect them against further injury. To do this, your opponent will have to drop his weapon. A solid eye shot is therefore an almost guaranteed fight stopper, whether delivered with a knife or with the fingers of the free hand. The eye socket is also the path of least resistance for direct attacks to the brain. The bone at the back of the eye sockets is much thinner than the outer plates of the skull and easily penetrated by a knife. This is an excellent quick-kill target.

• *Face.* The face is full of blood vessels, all located near the surface of the skin. If you've ever cut yourself shaving, you know how much a face cut can bleed. The physical damage caused by a face cut may not be great, but such a cut could still stop a fight because of the psychological shock it induces. The natural fear of disfigurement could be enough to prompt your opponent to cease and desist. This reaction should not be counted on, though, since it is equally possible that your landing such a cut will enrage your opponent.

• *Under the jaw.* The soft, fleshy area under the jaw is full of sensory and motor nerves that sense taste and control the mouth and tongue during speech. A knife thrust to this area will result in extreme pain, can send the tongue into spasms, and will spill large amounts of blood into the mouth and windpipe. A forceful upward thrust to this target could also penetrate the upper palate and reach the brain. Removal of the knife after such a thrust is difficult, however.

• *Under the ear.* If you press hard with your fingertip about an inch below your ear lobe and just behind the hinge of your jaw, you'll feel considerable pain. If you did the same with the point of a knife, the pain would be considerably greater. A thrust delivered at an upward angle at this point can also reach the brain, but you might need to stand on your opponent's head and pull with both hands to get your knife back.

• *Sides of the neck.* The actual targets are the external carotid arteries, which are located about 1.5 inches below the skin's surface on each side of the neck. These can be located by feeling your own pulse in your neck. Many people refer to "going for the jugular" when attacking the neck, but, as stated earlier, arteries are preferred targets to veins. The jugular is a vein. The exact position of the carotid arteries varies according to the angle at which the head is held. As the head tilts back, the arteries sink slightly deeper. A deep, powerful slash or thrust with a comma cut withdrawal is the best way to hit this target. In W.E. Fairbairn's book *Get Tough*, he included a table, known as "The Timetable of Death," that described exactly how long it would take for the average person to bleed, first to unconsciousness, then to death, if certain arteries were severed. The basis for his figures is unknown, but according to this table, a severed carotid artery will result in unconsciousness in as little as 5 seconds and death in 12.

• *Trachea (windpipe).* This target is located just below the larynx (Adam's apple) and above the collarbones. The trachea is not as heavily protected by cartilage as the larynx and therefore is more vulnerable. A thrust or powerful cut with a knife in this area can cut the trachea and spill blood into the windpipe and down into the lungs.

• *Subclavian artery.* Located about 2.5 inches beneath the notch between the clavicles (collarbones) and the trapezius muscle, this is a difficult target to hit. The best way of hitting it is to use a reverse grip to stab downward behind the collarbone. It is possible to do this with a standard grip as well, but it is much more difficult. Withdrawal of the knife after such a thrust is also tough. Despite the problems involved with attacking this target, it's still worth the trouble if you can pull it off. Once the subclavian artery is severed, your opponent will bleed to death, guaranteed. According to Fairbairn, this will take only 3.5 seconds.

• *Shoulder*. Although not a lethal target, a stab to the deltoid muscles of the shoulder can cause extreme pain and will affect the function of the entire arm.

• *Armpit*. The armpit is an excellent target, allowing access to the major artery and nerve bundle feeding the arm, as well as the lymph nodes. A stab to the armpit produces tremendous pain and will most likely cause at least temporary paralysis in the entire arm. A deep thrust could also damage the ligaments and tendons of the shoulder joint. The only disadvantage of striking this target is that withdrawing your blade can be tough.

• *Space between the biceps and triceps*. This target is located on the inside of the upper arm, between the biceps and triceps. At this point, the nerve bundle that runs down the arm is accessible. A quick thrust to this spot will produce intense pain and spasms in the arm, most likely disarming your opponent.

• *Base of the biceps*. This target is located on the upper side of the hollow of the arm opposite the elbow. Approximately half an inch below the surface of the skin in this spot is the brachial artery and the cubital fossa, which is the attachment of the tendon of the biceps muscle to the forearm. According to Fairbairn, severing the brachial artery will render a person unconscious in 14 seconds and result in death in 1 1/2 minutes. Severing the cubital fossa disconnects the biceps from the forearm and makes flexing the arm impossible.

• *Forearm/wrist*. Any cut to the forearm or wrist can have a debilitating effect, but cuts to the inside surface of the wrist are best. Approximately 1/4 inch below the skin of the wrist is the radial artery. You can find its exact location by feeling your own pulse. This is the artery that most would-be suicides try to cut, often without success because they fail to cut

deep enough. The "Timetable of Death" indicates that completely severing the radial artery will result in unconsciousness in 30 seconds and death in 2 minutes. By cutting a little deeper, you can also sever the tendons that link the muscles of the forearm with the fingers. These are plainly visible if you look at your wrist and wiggle your fingers. If these are cut, the hand can no longer grasp anything, and your opponent is disarmed instantly. A less effective, but still worthwhile alternative, is to cut the muscles in the forearm that control the fingers. The result is the same: the hand is rendered useless and can no longer hold a weapon.

• *Fingers*. Another method of disarming an attacker is to cut or chop off the fingers of his weapon hand. This often happens unintentionally when aiming for a wrist cut. You either misjudge the distance or your opponent realizes he is about to be cut and tries to withdraw his hand. His fingers are caught between your blade and the handle of his knife, ruining his day and most likely taking him out of the fight. Finger cuts can also be applied against his free hand, either offensively while his hand is dangling out front or defensively as he tries to punch or grab with it.

• *Lungs*. Any thrust to the chest or rib cage has the potential of puncturing the pleural membranes surrounding the lungs. These membranes surround each lung and also line the inside of the chest cavity around each lung. Normally, the two membranes around each lung are in close contact with each other and are completely sealed. When the chest expands, the outer pleura expands with it. The air-tight seal between the membranes then causes the inner membrane and the lung to expand as well, inflating the lung. A knife wound that punctures the pleura breaks the seal between the two membranes and allows air to fill the space in between. This causes a condition called pneumothorax, or more commonly, a sucking chest wound. The air drawn into the chest cavity through the wound causes the lung to deflate, seriously impairing your opponent's ability to breathe. A deep thrust can puncture the lung as well, further impairing the breathing and filling the lung with blood. This condition can easily result in death if first aid is not rendered quickly.

• *Diaphragm*. The diaphragm is the sheet of muscle beneath the front of the rib cage in the area of the solar plexus. It is the primary muscle involved in respiration. A knife wound through this muscle will seriously impair your opponent's ability to breathe and may also puncture the pleural membranes. The result, like that of the sucking chest wound, is ultimately oxygen deprivation leading to collapse and possible death.

• *Heart*. The heart can be reached by knife thrusts directed inward through the intercostal spaces (the spaces between the ribs) in the area of the third, fourth, and fifth ribs or by a thrust angled upward under the sternum. As mentioned earlier, any thrusts between the ribs can make withdrawing your blade difficult. Also, these thrusts require much greater precision to avoid hitting bone, especially when heavy clothing is worn. A thrust angled upward under the rib cage is easier to deliver and recover from, but requires a knife with a blade at least 5 inches long, more if your opponent is obese. For maximum effect when using an upward thrust, the blade should be moved from side to side to increase the size of the wound channel before withdrawing it with a comma cut. Once the heart is punctured, your opponent will drop quickly and expire with great haste (and mess).

• *Spleen*. The spleen is a major blood-filled organ located on the left side of the body at a level about even with the floating ribs. A knife thrust under the floating ribs in this location or one angling from the center of the body outward to the left side can puncture the spleen and result in serious bleeding.

• *Liver*. The liver is located on the right side of the body, about 4 inches to the right of the solar plexus. Like the spleen, it is constantly filled with blood. A knife thrust aimed under or through the ribs or angling outward to the right from the center of the body can tear or puncture the liver and the blood vessels that supply it, resulting in severe bleeding.

• *Abdominal aorta/vena cava*. The major artery and vein (respectively) supplying and collecting blood from the abdomen and lower body, these blood vessels lie just in front of the spine. A deep thrust into the abdomen can puncture one or both of them, but by moving the knife blade horizontally from side to side, you increase your chances of severing them. If successful, be prepared for a virtual fountain of blood and make any derogatory comments about your opponent quickly, as he won't be alive very long to hear them.

• *Bladder*. Even a shallow thrust to the bladder area a few inches above the genitals will produce extreme pain because of the dense concentration of nerves in this area.

• *Groin*. Any knife slash, cut, or thrust to the genitals can result in extreme pain, profuse bleeding, and tremendous psychological shock because of fear of disfigurement. Even if your knife does not penetrate the clothing (very possible if your opponent is wearing jeans or other heavy pants), the impact of the blow will have a telling effect on men and will still produce psychological shock.

• *Spot between the anus and the groin*. Although a difficult target to reach in a stand-up fight, it is very accessible if you find yourself in a headlock. This area contains a concentration of nerves for the entire groin area. A knife thrust will produce tremendous pain and will probably put your opponent on the ground instantly. Knife withdrawal is typically tough, though, because of the body's natural tendency to curl up in the fetal position when so stuck.

• *Femoral artery/nerves on inside of the thigh*. This target is located on the inside of the thigh, just below the fold where the thigh meets the abdomen. A knife thrust to this area can strike the femoral artery, the femoral vein, and the femoral nerve. The former two will bleed profusely when cut and may result in death because of the difficulty in stopping the bleeding from such a wound. Damage to the latter will prevent or seriously impair any coordinated movement of that leg and may cause collapse.

• *Knee*. Deep cuts anywhere around the knee joint can sever the connecting tissues that support the joint and either impair its mobility or cause collapse. A solid side, front, or stomping kick to the knee joint will also break it, putting your opponent on the ground and most likely ending the fight.

• *Shin.* The concentration of nerves immediately below the skin of the shin makes any strike or cut to this area very painful. The opportunity for such cuts usually only presents itself when your opponent attempts a kick.

REAR TARGETS

The targets located on the back of the body that are vulnerable to knife attacks include the following:

• *Base of skull.* The exact location is the slight depression between the two tendons that can be felt on either side of the spine at the base of the neck. The actual target is the spinal cord and the medulla oblongata, the lower rear portion of the brain. The brain and spinal cord form the center of the nervous system. If they were suddenly separated from each other, death would be instantaneous. Your opponent would not even hear the sound of his own body hitting the ground. A partial severing of the spinal cord in this area would result in major paralysis and possibly still cause death. This is an extremely difficult target to hit with a knife thrust, but it can be done. A simpler method is to use a large, heavy knife or machete and chop into this area.

• *Triceps muscle/back of the elbow.* The target here is the triceps muscle itself or, preferably, the tendons that connect it to the forearm. The muscle is easily found at the back of the arm. A deep cut will sever enough muscle tissue and generate sufficient pain to severely impair or disable the arm. Between the triceps and the point of the elbow are the tendons that attach it to the forearm. If these are cut, the triceps can no longer move the forearm, and the arm is effectively disabled.

• *Kidneys.* Located close to the surface of the skin just below the floating ribs and several inches to either side of the spine are the kidneys. They are very sensitive, full of blood at all times, and supplied with blood by large vessels that are also vulnerable to damage if the organ is attacked. A knife thrust to the kidney will cause extreme pain and bleeding and will probably end the fight.

• *Back of the thigh.* A thrust to the back of the thigh just below the fold of the buttock could

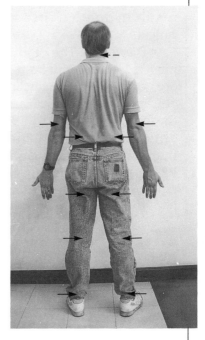

The knife targets located on the back of the body.

strike the sciatic nerve, which controls coordinated movements of the leg. This largest nerve in the body, if hit, will cause great pain and seriously impair the mobility of the leg and your opponent's ability to stand. Deep cuts or thrusts lower on the back of the thigh will damage the hamstring muscle, yielding similar results.

• *Back of the knee.* A thrust or deep cut to the back of the knee can damage the nerves of the leg as well as the tendons and ligaments that support that joint. The pain and damage to the physical structures could cause that leg to collapse.

• *Achilles tendon.* This is the tendon that connects the calf muscle to the foot, allowing the foot to flex and support weight. It is clearly visible at the back of the ankle. If severed, that leg will no longer be able to support any weight, and your opponent will either have to continue the fight on one leg or will collapse to his knees. This target is difficult to cut in a stand-up fight, but is vulnerable if your opponent attempts a kick and during grappling.

These targets are the ones most vulnerable to an attack with a knife. By learning their locations and the physiological effects of knife attacks to these areas, you can make the best of every cut or thrust you deliver in a fight and bring an end to the fight as quickly as possible.

EFFECT OF CLOTHING ON TARGETING

One thing you must consider when selecting targets during a fight, however, is your opponent's clothing. Certain types of clothing and

 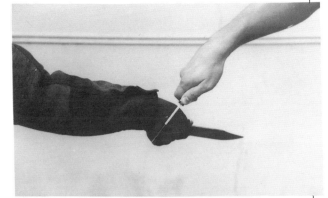

The type of clothing your attacker wears affects the targets you have available to you. Leather jackets and similar items of clothing are tough to cut and should be passed up in favor of exposed or lightly covered targets. Similarly, if you happen to be wearing a leather jacket, you might save yourself some stitches.

materials are surprisingly resistant to being cut or punctured with a knife. If the target you are aiming at happens to lie beneath such an article of clothing, you had best look for another target rather than waste a cut or thrust.

For example, in your knife-fighting practice, you may get used to cutting your opponent's forearm when doing meets, passes, and follows. The forearm is, after all, a bigger target than the wrist and therefore easier to hit. However, this only works if your opponent is wearing a short-sleeve shirt or a light long-sleeve shirt or jacket. A heavy leather jacket can provide great protection against slashes, especially with small knives. If an attacker on the street happens to be wearing such a jacket, you'll need to adapt and go for unprotected targets. Your meets, passes, and follows will now have to be directed at his hand and the small exposed portion of his wrist. Thrusts to the body are also out and should be redirected to the neck and head or targets below the waist.

Denim jeans are another type of material

that can resist knife attacks surprisingly well. To determine how well your carry knife will cut or penetrate denim, take an old pair of jeans (not too ragged, as they will give you deceptive results), make a cylindrical roll out of cardboard boxes about the size of your thigh, and put it inside. Then set it up and try a few practice cuts and thrusts. Watch the results carefully and note which techniques work best. Notice the difference in penetration when the cloth is loosely draped over the target as opposed to tightly stretched. Finally file your observations in your mind and be ready to adapt instantly when you face an opponent wearing hard-to-cut clothing.

While doing your tests, you should also take a look at your own wardrobe and see which articles of clothing might protect you from the effects of a knife attack. By selecting items like leather jackets or military field jackets, jeans, and leather gloves, you can literally provide yourself with a light coat of armor and increase your chances of survival in a knife fight.

CHAPTER TEN

Example Techniques

he techniques demonstrated in this chapter are examples of typical offensive and defensive techniques that can be used in a knife fight. Note that I said *examples*.

OFFENSIVE TECHNIQUES

The following offensive techniques demonstrate applications of offensive footwork integrated with effective cutting and thrusting techniques and the use of natural body weapons. Practice them first exactly as you see them presented here. If a certain technique doesn't flow or feel right for you, try to modify it until it does. Adjust the footwork or vary the targets to make it fit your personal style of fighting. Then examine the result critically to find any weaknesses or vulnerabilities. If it works for you and doesn't leave you open to being cut or hit, practice it until it becomes reflex.

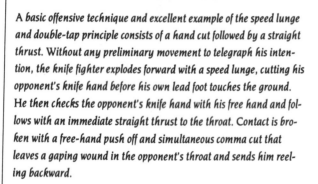

A basic offensive technique and excellent example of the speed lunge and double-tap principle consists of a hand cut followed by a straight thrust. Without any preliminary movement to telegraph his intention, the knife fighter explodes forward with a speed lunge, cutting his opponent's knife hand before his own lead foot touches the ground. He then checks the opponent's knife hand with his free hand and follows with an immediate straight thrust to the throat. Contact is broken with a free-hand push off and simultaneous comma cut that leaves a gaping wound in the opponent's throat and sends him reeling backward.

If your opponent tries to attack with a backhand slash, you can seize the initiative and go on the offensive before he can follow through. As he cocks his arm back, explode forward and cut his triceps. Immediately, safety check the back of his elbow to control his arm and follow with a thrust to the groin or inner thigh. Do a comma cut and push off to break contact.

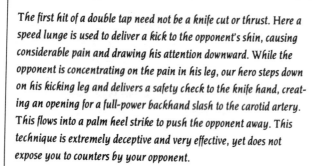

The first hit of a double tap need not be a knife cut or thrust. Here a speed lunge is used to deliver a kick to the opponent's shin, causing considerable pain and drawing his attention downward. While the opponent is concentrating on the pain in his leg, our hero steps down on his kicking leg and delivers a safety check to the knife hand, creating an opening for a full-power backhand slash to the carotid artery. This flows into a palm heel strike to push the opponent away. This technique is extremely deceptive and very effective, yet does not expose you to counters by your opponent.

Sometimes a feint (false attack) can be used to create an opening for an offensive double tap. Here the knife fighter feints an attack at his opponent's lead leg to prompt him to lower his guard. When he does, it leaves him open for a free-hand finger jab to the eyes. The blinded opponent drops his knife and instinctively covers his eyes, leaving him wide open for an optional fight- (and life-) stopping thrust to the throat.

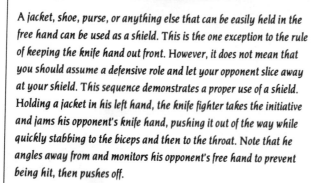

A jacket, shoe, purse, or anything else that can be easily held in the free hand can be used as a shield. This is the one exception to the rule of keeping the knife hand out front. However, it does not mean that you should assume a defensive role and let your opponent slice away at your shield. This sequence demonstrates a proper use of a shield. Holding a jacket in his left hand, the knife fighter takes the initiative and jams his opponent's knife hand, pushing it out of the way while quickly stabbing to the biceps and then to the throat. Note that he angles away from and monitors his opponent's free hand to prevent being hit, then pushes off.

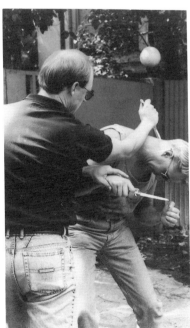

This sequence illustrates how the reverse grip can be used to deliver a surprise attack. Held in this grip, the knife is concealed from the opponent's view by the forearm. When the opponent threatens with a weapon of his own, the knife fighter takes the initiative and executes an inward slash to the throat while simultaneously checking the opponent's knife hand and angling away from his blade. The slash leaves the knife fighter's hand cocked for a follow-up backhand thrust to the opposite side of the neck or base of the skull to end the fight.

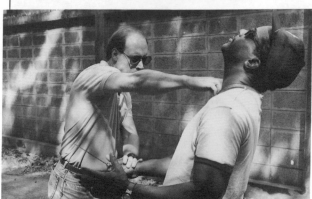

Here our knife fighter is surprised by an attacker and has not yet drawn his blade. To buy time and distance to do so, he fakes compliance, then punches the attacker in the throat while checking his knife hand. He then quickly backs away and draws his own knife, ready to continue the fight if necessary. Note that he keeps his left hand out front while drawing his knife. If the fight were to continue, he would, of course, assume a knife-forward stance.

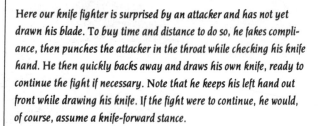

DEFENSIVE TECHNIQUES

The techniques in the following sequences demonstrate some applications of the various defensive principles and concepts discussed in this book. They combine defensive footwork with the defensive responses, body angling, and a variety of counter cuts and thrusts to give you an idea of what effective defenses should look like. They are not intended to be the last word on knife defense. Practice them, modify them, and use the principles that make them work to develop your own techniques and methods.

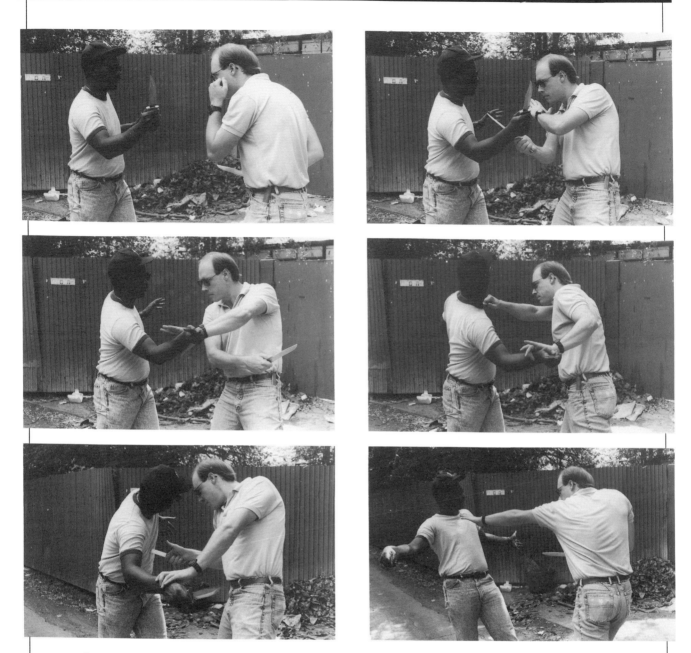

Against a high inward-slashing attack to zone one, the knife fighter steps diagonally forward to his right and executes a meet to the attacker's wrist. This is quickly followed by a safety check to stop the knife hand and a backhand slash to the neck. If time and circumstances allow, a straight thrust to the chest is added, followed by a comma cut and push off. If there isn't time for the final thrust, push off immediately after slashing.

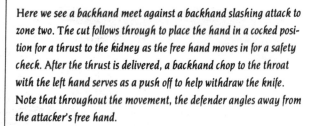

Here we see a backhand meet against a backhand slashing attack to zone two. The cut follows through to place the hand in a cocked position for a thrust to the kidney as the free hand moves in for a safety check. After the thrust is delivered, a backhand chop to the throat with the left hand serves as a push off to help withdraw the knife. Note that throughout the movement, the defender angles away from the attacker's free hand.

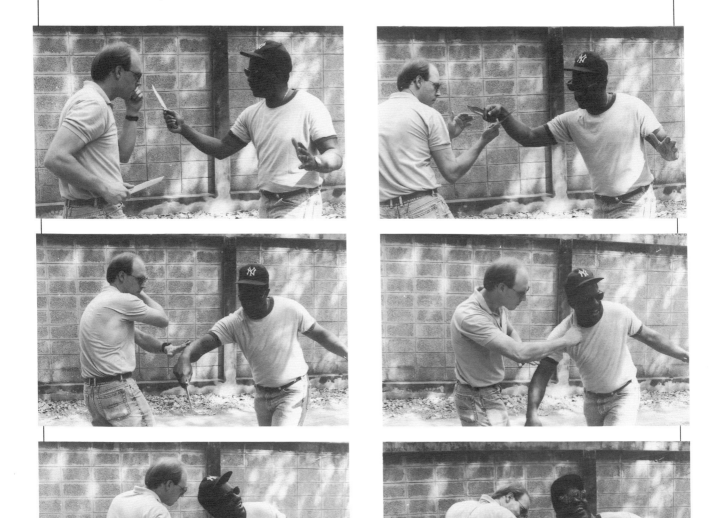

Here is an application of a pass against a high slash to zone one. The knife hand is out and allowed to continue its arc so the knife fighter can move in behind it. The left hand checks the knife hand, keeping it from snapping back for a backhand cut, while the knife fighter executes an abanico backhand/forehand cut combination to the neck, giving his attacker a toothless smile from ear to ear.

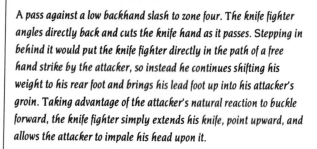

A pass against a low backhand slash to zone four. The knife fighter angles directly back and cuts the knife hand as it passes. Stepping in behind it would put the knife fighter directly in the path of a free hand strike by the attacker, so instead he continues shifting his weight to his rear foot and brings his lead foot up into his attacker's groin. Taking advantage of the attacker's natural reaction to buckle forward, the knife fighter simply extends his knife, point upward, and allows the attacker to impale his head upon it.

Here's an example of a follow, again a low-slashing attack to zone three. The knife fighter slides back slightly to avoid the incoming blade but remains close enough to cut the back of the attacker's hand after it passes. Springing forward, he continues the momentum of his knife hand and flows into an inward slash to the neck.

The defensive responses against an attack to zone five are less clear-cut than for other zones and tend to look the same. Only slight differences in angle and timing separate a meet from a pass or follow. Here our knife fighter steps diagonally to the side to evade a straight thrust to the abdomen. At the same time, he executes a cutting deflection to the attacker's knife hand. He then follows with a powerful upper cut-style straight upward thrust under the attacker's chin. He finishes the technique by stepping forward and executing a leaping leg throw. The thrusting motion of the knife is continued throughout the throw to unbalance the opponent and ensure maximum penetration. Done properly, this is a sure killing technique.

Downward stabbing attacks, a la Psycho, are rarely as telegraphed as in the movies. Instead, short, hard-to-block arcs are the norm. A standard cutting-style defensive response is possible against this attack but leaves little opportunity for a follow-up cut or thrust. A different solution is demonstrated here. Rather than cutting first, the knife forearm and the free hand are used together to deflect the stab and continue its momentum. As our knife hand comes around in its arc, turn the deflection into a thrust with both blades, driving them into your attacker's groin or thighs. While he is contemplating his career as a falsetto in the choir, withdraw your knife and take advantage of his natural reaction to jackknife forward by delivering an uppercut-style straight thrust into his throat or under his chin.

Here an attacker opens with a kick. If it were aimed low, it would be best to dodge it or block it with your foot rather than try to cut it, since that would leave your upper body dangerously exposed. Here the kick is aimed at the groin or stomach. Don't try to cut the leg directly, since the power of a kick may dislodge your knife. Instead, take an angular step to get you out of the path of the kick and deflect the attacker's leg with your knife-hand forearm. As you follow through, turn the deflection into a slash to the Achilles tendon. As the attacker steps down onto his kicking leg, continue to angle to his outside and finish him with a straight thrust to the kidney.

Here's an example of the use of the reverse grip. As your attacker throws a straight thrust, step diagonally to your left with your left foot to get out the line of attack. Hook his knife wrist with the blade of your knife and slam your elbow into the back of his elbow. Done properly and with sufficient power, this will break his arm and make him drop his knife. Slap his arm downward with your left hand and immediately execute an inward slash to his throat.

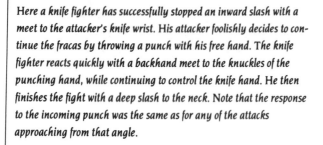

Here a knife fighter has successfully stopped an inward slash with a meet to the attacker's knife wrist. His attacker foolishly decides to continue the fracas by throwing a punch with his free hand. The knife fighter reacts quickly with a backhand meet to the knuckles of the punching hand, while continuing to control the knife hand. He then finishes the fight with a deep slash to the neck. Note that the response to the incoming punch was the same as for any of the attacks approaching from that angle.

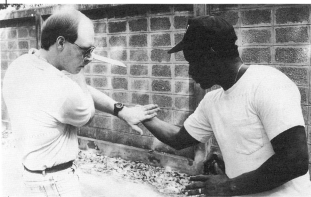

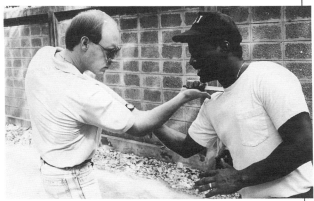

Here is another example of a defense against a thrust to zone five. The straight thrust is deflected with a point-drawn inward slash to the wrist and immediately followed by a safety check with the left hand. The follow-through of the deflection leaves the knife hand coiled for a backhand angular thrust to the neck. A push off and comma cut complete the technique.

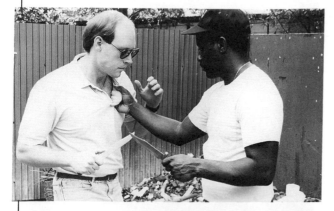

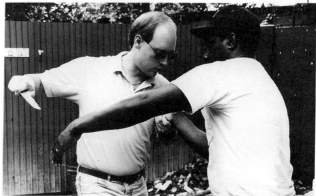

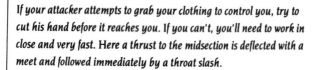

If your attacker attempts to grab your clothing to control you, try to cut his hand before it reaches you. If you can't, you'll need to work in close and very fast. Here a thrust to the midsection is deflected with a meet and followed immediately by a throat slash.

CHAPTER ELEVEN

Counterdefenses

A counterdefense is a technique that is designed to counter or overcome your opponent's defensive actions. More simply, if you try to cut your opponent and he is able to block it, a counterdefense allows you to immediately react and cut him before he can mount another defense.

Most counterdefenses begin with your opponent blocking or checking your knife arm with his hand or arm. When this happens, the natural reaction is to struggle and apply additional pressure to try to push your knife past his arm to the target. Wrong answer.

First of all, your chances of success in getting past your opponent's defending arm are poor. He stopped you once and has a good chance of continuing to stop you from getting in. Secondly, if he blocked with his free hand, his weapon hand is still lurking out there somewhere. If you get too preoccupied with trying to force a failed technique to work, you won't be able to react to your opponent's attacks. Finally, although your opponent blocked one cut, in doing so, he left himself open to be cut in another way which he will probably not expect or be able to prevent.

If your opponent should happen to block one of your attacks, you should apply an immediate counterdefense. Here an opponent successfully blocks an inward slash. The knife fighter immediately checks the opponent's blocking arm with his free hand to hold it in place, then pulls his knife hand straight back to slash it. At the completion of the slash, the hand is cocked and ready to execute a straight thrust to the throat.

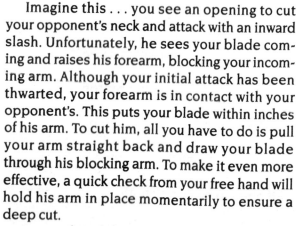

Imagine this . . . you see an opening to cut your opponent's neck and attack with an inward slash. Unfortunately, he sees your blade coming and raises his forearm, blocking your incoming arm. Although your initial attack has been thwarted, your forearm is in contact with your opponent's. This puts your blade within inches of his arm. To cut him, all you have to do is pull your arm straight back and draw your blade through his blocking arm. To make it even more effective, a quick check from your free hand will hold his arm in place momentarily to ensure a deep cut.

Remember the comma cut? It basically consisted of turning your hand over from palm up to palm down (or vice versa) while cutting a nasty little arc out of a wound channel you just made in your opponent's body. Well, imagine this . . . you attempt a backhanded angular thrust. Your opponent is too quick, however, and checks your forearm with the palm of his free hand. Rather than struggle with him to try to push your knife toward the original target, quickly pat his checking hand with your own free hand and do a comma cut motion with your knife hand. This will turn your hand over from palm up to palm down and from a backhanded thrust position to a backhanded slash position.

Here a backhand angular thrust is blocked by the opponent's free hand. The knife fighter immediately checks the opponent's blocking hand to hold it in place and rotates his knife hand with the same motion as used with a comma cut. As the knife hand rotates downward, it places the edge of the knife in perfect position to deliver a deep slash to the wrist. The checking hand continues to apply pressure to the blocking hand, moving it out of the way and creating an opening for a follow-up inward angular thrust to the neck.

It will also place the edge of your blade against the wrist of your opponent's checking arm. The comma cut movement flows into a short backhand slash and your opponent's career as a piano player is over forever.

The counterdefense for a blocked inward angular thrust is a mirror image of the one for the backhand thrust. In this case your checking hand pushes to your right and your knife hand turns from palm down to palm up to execute an inward slash to the wrist.

If you happen to have a double-edged knife or one with a sharpened false edge, you can often cut your opponent by pulling straight back without having to turn your hand over.

Counterdefenses should be practiced with a partner until they become automatic. As soon as you feel your knife hand stopped by your opponent's hand or arm, you should flow automatically into a counterdefense without hesitation. In addition to allowing you to undermine your opponent's defenses and cut his arm, you'll note that, upon completion, counterdefenses place your knife hand in a perfect cocked position to continue your attack on another angle. When a counterdefense is done in conjunction with a safety check, your checking hand will not only stabilize your opponent's arm while you cut it, sustained pressure will push it out of the way to create an opening for your follow up.

In knife fighting, like any martial art, for every counter there is yet another counter. While it is unlikely that the typical blade-wielding street punk will have read this book or know how to execute a counterdefense, you need to protect yourself against such moves when you block or check your opponent's blade. The way to do this when checking with your free hand is to be aware of any movements of your attacker's knife hand while you're in contact with it. Develop a sensitivity while checking so that, if you sense that his knife hand is moving to cut your checking hand, you

In some cases, you may be forced to block a cut or thrust with the forearm of your knife hand. If this happens, turn it from a defensive move into an offensive one by pulling your forearm slightly back and snapping it downward sharply to cut your attacker's knife hand. This move also protects you from getting cut if your attacker is smart and quick enough to try a counterdefense.

execute a meet to cut your opponent's knife hand, block his knife arm with the outside of your forearm. Then, to avoid getting cut and to slip in one of your own, immediately withdraw your hand slightly and cut straight down at his knife arm. Even if he is quick and tries a counterdefensive cut, you'll still have a good chance of cutting his hand as his blade is slicing through the air where *your* hand was just a fraction of a second before. If you block a cut thrown at a low level, your blade point will probably be facing down. In this case, withdraw your hand and cut upward.

Another application of counterdefenses is when your knife wrist is grabbed by your opponent. Again rather than struggling against the

can either withdraw your hand from the path of his blade or push his knife hand away quickly. By making your free hand blocks and checks snappy movements rather than sustained pushes, you also minimize your chances of falling victim to a counterdefensive cut.

Sometimes you will find yourself forced to block with your knife-hand forearm. If you are caught in a tight situation and are unable to

strength of his grasp, your aim is to react immediately with a proper technique, forcing a release by cutting him.

If your knife hand is grabbed, unless your opponent's grasp is close to your hand, you will still have considerable wrist mobility and will be able to bring your blade to bear against his wrist. There are several ways of doing this.

The first method is to straighten your wrist

One way to make your opponent let go after grabbing your knife wrist is to bend your knees slightly, drop your knife-arm elbow, and punch forward at an upward diagonal angle. This will put the edge of your blade straight into the inside of his wrist. If the pain of the cutting isn't enough to make him let go, once you slice deep enough to sever the tendons that work his fingers, he'll have no choice but to loosen his grasp, permanently. Note that once the knife hand is freed, it is snapped outward, drawing the full edge across the wrist for a deep cut.

so your blade is perpendicular to your forearm. Now bend your arm slightly at the elbow, bend your knees, and punch your knife hand at an upward angle straight toward your opponent. This will bring the edge of the blade directly against the inside of his wrist and in perfect position to cut his radial artery and the tendons that lead to his fingers. The longer and tighter he hangs on, the deeper you will cut. If he doesn't let go because of the pain or the realization that he is being cut, his grasp will eventually loosen as the tendons are cut and the fingers rendered useless. If you feel his grip loosening and your knife hand coming free, make the best of the opportunity and quickly do a backhand slash, drawing the full length of your blade edge across his wrist to cut as deep as possible. The only disadvantage to this tactic is that it can leave you vulnerable to the blade held in his other hand. To minimize your risk, you can step diagonally to his outside away

from his blade hand and use his grasping arm as an obstacle to keep from getting cut.

A variation of this technique is to stick the point of your knife into the fleshy underside of his forearm and then thrust upward. This will probably drive the knife right through his forearm and, in the process, break his grip. To finish the job, pull your blade sharply downward to cut his forearm all the way to the elbow. This creates a spectacular bleeding wound and helps free your blade. The only problem with this move is that it's hard to do with long-bladed knives.

A wrist grab release that requires a bit more finesse involves rotating your knife hand to place the blade point up on either side of your opponent's hand, then cutting sideways into his wrist to break his grip. This works well if done quickly, but if your opponent figures out what you're doing and has a strong grip, you may have trouble making it work. If you are

Another way of dealing with a wrist grab is to use a similar motion, but place the point of the knife against the fleshy underside of your opponent's arm, effecting a release. When he lets go, free your blade with a downward pulling cut that will open his forearm all the way to the elbow. As with all releases, monitor your attacker's knife hand and be prepared to defend against it with your free hand. These photos are staged for clarity, so the attacker obediently refrains from trying to use his knife. In a real fight, he wouldn't be so polite.

using a single-edged knife, you can get extra power in this technique by pushing with the palm of your free hand against the back of the blade. Once again, if you feel your opponent's grip begin to loosen, snap your hand downward and draw the entire length of your blade edge across his wrist for a good, deep cut. Like the techniques described above, this one is safest if you step or pivot to your opponent's outside on the side away from his weapon hand.

One very simple and often overlooked release that can be used when your knife hand is grabbed is to just switch your knife to your other hand. While your opponent is still hanging on to your now empty former weapon hand (an action which, as stupid as it seems, is completely natural), you can start carving his hand off of yours or go straight for a more vulnerable target.

If you happen to be holding your knife in a reverse grip when your wrist is grabbed, you can still apply the latter two release techniques

described above: rotating your knife hand to cut your opponent's wrist or passing the knife to your other hand. You also have a third option that is only possible with a reverse grip. Using your free hand, trap your opponent's grabbing hand to your own wrist. Now rotate your knife around in the direction of *the back of your opponent's wrist*. In other words, if he grabbed your right wrist with his right hand, you'll rotate your hand clockwise. If he grabbed with his left hand, you'll rotate counterclockwise. Now hook your blade over the back of his wrist, step back slightly (at the same time angling away from his knife hand), and pull down. This creates a painful wristlock that will bring your attacker to his knees. If you have a double-edged knife, you're also cutting deeply into the back of his wrist. Once you've got him down, continue to monitor his knife hand and quickly administer a solid kick to his groin. This won't be as difficult as it would be normally since his groin will

A wrist grab can also be broken by rotating your hand to either side of your opponent's wrist, pointing your blade upward and exerting side pressure to simultaneously cut his wrist and lever out of his grip. If your are using a single-edged knife, you can back it with your free hand to apply greater pressure. As always, the move ends by drawing the full edge of the blade across the target to cut as deep as possible.

One simple solution to a hand grab is to put your free hand to work and poke your opponent in the eyes. He will release your wrist—and most likely drop his weapon as well—as he instinctively covers his eyes with his hands. This of course leaves his helpless to defend against any follow-up strikes. Note here that the knife fighter angles away from the attacker's weapon hand just in case he is able to retain his knife after he's a hit.

only be about a foot off the floor. While he's rethinking his family-planning program, you can finish with any number of powerful downward stabs to his exposed back. Targets that come to mind include the base of the skull, the kidneys, and, if he's not writhing around too much to spoil your aim, the subclavian artery.

Whenever your knife hand is grabbed, don't forget you still have your natural body weapons as well. A finger jab to the eyes with your free hand will automatically break your opponent's grip and leave him open for you to finish the job with your knife. Remember, *knife fighting is a total body endeavor!*

CHAPTER TWELVE

Training Drills and Apparatuses

The only way to develop any amount of skill in fighting with a knife is to practice the concepts and techniques described in this book with a partner. To do so safely, you'll need to obtain some proper training equipment. Fortunately, this is a cheap and easy proposition.

TRAINING KNIVES

The first thing you'll need, obviously, is a couple of training knives. A training knife can be made out of a variety of materials, ranging from hollow plastic to unsharpened steel.

Rubber Knives

The easiest way to get started is to purchase some rubber knives from a martial arts supply store. These knives are a realistic size and are made of a flexible rubber that will flex on contact to prevent injury. If you don't have a martial arts supply store in your area, the local toy store will often have hol-

Shown here are some of the types of training knives that can be used to practice knife fighting. They include homemade rubber knives made from foam rubber typewriter pads, commercial rubber training knives, commercial wooden knives, homemade wooden knives, and homemade aluminum knives.

low plastic toy knives that can be used. These are a bit light, however, and are not as desirable as the rubber type.

If you want top-of-the-line rubber training knives with a realistic balance, Al Mar Knives makes rubber training knives based on the design of the Applegate-Fairbairn Fighting Knife. Although a bit pricey at about $20 a pair, they are a great training aid.

Plastic Knives

Plastic knives are acceptable for most training scenarios and are especially good for beginners. However, as you get more advanced, you need to practice with something more realistic so that it stings a little when you get hit. This will help condition you to the pain inherent in knife fighting and really let you know when you would have suffered a serious cut if the fighting had been for real. Also, a rigid practice knife is needed to practice some techniques, such as wrist grab defenses.

Wooden Knives

The next most common type of training knife is made of wood. A whack with a wooden knife will certainly let you know when you would have gotten cut. However, you don't necessarily need to suffer a broken arm to come to such a realization. The wooden training knives sold in most martial arts supply stores are patterned after the traditional Japanese tanto

knife and are constructed like *bokken*, Japanese hardwood training swords. While the weight of these knives adds a certain amount of realism, I don't enjoy training with them.

A better alternative is to make your own wooden knife. Practically any type of soft or hard wood can be used. You can either whittle it out by hand, use hand woodworking tools, or use power tools. The advantage of handmade practice knives is that they tend to feel more like real knives than the commercial wooden knives. In fact, with a little patience and skill, you can make a wooden replica of your actual fighting knife to add a greater element of realism to your training. You can also make a variety of knives with blades of different lengths so you can get used to picking up practically any style of knife and fighting with it.

Aluminum Knives

If you're really ambitious, great practice knives can be made from aluminum bar stock, which is available at very reasonable prices at most hardware stores. The bar stock can be shaped with files and sandpaper to resemble a knife blade and then fitted with a handle in exactly the same manner as a real knife. The metallic look of these knives makes them appear very much like actual knives, adding an extra element of realism to practice sessions.

If you choose to make your own training knives, make safety paramount in their design. Ensure that the point of the knife is sufficiently rounded to prevent puncture wounds. Also, sand the blades and handles to make them smooth and rounded. This will prevent cuts and splinters during training.

Using Real Knives to Practice

The ultimate training knife is to take an actual fighting knife and dull the blade and point. Although more expensive than any other type of practice knife, it is the most realistic. In addition to giving you the exact feel and balance of your combat knife, it allows you to practice other aspects of knife fighting, such as drawing your knife quickly, and integrate them into your technique practice. This is of particular value if your primary fighting knife is a folder, since you can practice drawing, opening,

The padded stick is an excellent training tool that allows you to practice full-power cuts with a live blade and get used to the feel of hard contact. The more realistic you can make your training, the better you'll be able to survive when the real thing happens to you.

and fighting with it the same way you would in a real situation.

You may be tempted to simply tape the edge and point of your favorite fighting blade and use it for training. Don't! Even when heavily taped, the sharp edge of a knife has a way of peeking out and cutting when you least expect it. If you can't afford to buy a second fighting knife to dull to use for training, make one out of another material.

TRAINING DRILLS

Now that you have your basic equipment and a basic understanding of the concepts of knife fighting, you can begin to refine your skills and develop your reflexes with a few training drills. These drills are not designed as fighting techniques. Obviously nobody is going to stand there and continue to attack you after you've sliced his knife arm seven times in a row. The purpose of these drills is to develop your timing, reflexes, and ability to judge distance. After endless hours of such training, the *individual* movements that comprise the entire drill become second nature. At that point, when you see a knife swinging your way, you'll react quickly and properly without having to calculate your response.

Defensive Responses

The first drill is designed to practice the defensive responses. We'll start with the meet. You and your partner should begin by assuming guard stances a few feet apart. In this drill, your partner will be the attacker and you will be the defender. At *a slow speed*, have your partner begin throwing slashing attacks at you with a training knife, pausing between each cut. As you see each of his cuts coming toward you, execute a meet to simulate cutting his knife hand and follow it with a safety check. Continue the drill, having him throw one cut after another for you to defend against. Start easy, having him attack the five zones in order. Then, as you get better, have him mix his attacks, hitting different zones with a variety of cuts and thrusts. Later, have him vary not only the type of attack, but its speed and tempo. He can also incorporate feints to challenge your ability to react only to real attacks.

Again, start slow to develop proper technique. Going too fast will make you sloppy and develop bad habits. As your skill increases, gradually increase speed. Throughout this exercise, your feet should not move more than a few inches from your initial stance. Later, as you get better, do the exercise on the move to incorporate footwork and body angling.

After practicing meets for a while and switching off to give your partner a chance to cut on you, do the same drill for passes and follows. Remember to start slow and follow each defensive response with an appropriate safety check. Progress in speed, variety, and mobility as described for the previous drill.

Double-Tap Drills

The next drill is called the double-tap drill.

As its name indicates, it is used to develop the ability to deliver double taps quickly and fluidly. This drill begins just like the previous drills. The difference is that, after you do your initial hand cut and safety check, you follow instantly with an attack to a major target. For example, against an inward slash, you may do a meet to the inside of your partner's wrist, then a safety check, and follow with a backhand slash to the neck. This drill will not only teach you to use cuts and thrusts in combination, it will get you thinking about specific body targets and how to attack them. You'll find that defensive responses executed at certain levels leave your knife hand in position and your opponent open for specific follow-up attacks to major targets. A meet done against a high-level backhand slash, for example, leaves your knife hand cocked near your right ribs and your opponent's entire right side from armpit to hip wide open. What target(s) would you hit? Practicing this drill will teach you. As always, start this drill slowly and in a stationary position. As you get better, increase your speed and mobility to make it more realistic.

Counterdefense Drill

Another useful drill is the counterdefense drill. In this drill, you are the aggressor. You attack your partner with a variety of cuts and thrusts. His job is to block them with his empty hand or the forearm of his knife hand. Each time he blocks, you should immediately execute a counterdefensive action to cut his arm. Straight pullbacks and comma cuts combined with timely safety checks are the tools you'll use here. After you get proficient at doing the counterdefenses alone, practice combining them with a follow-up cut or thrust as you would in a real fight. This drill is particularly valuable in developing the ability to flow from one offensive technique to another quickly and not lose your composure when one of your attacks happens to be blocked.

A variation of the counterdefense drill helps you practice your counters against hand grabs. Instead of just blocking your cuts and thrusts, your partner will grab your wrist. Your response should be to immediately apply one of the counters described in the chapter on counter-

defenses, while angling away from your partner's knife hand and, if necessary, defending against his cuts and thrusts.

To practice defending with your knife-hand forearm, try this drill. Have your partner throw slashes and thrusts at you. Each time, block his knife-hand forearm with the outside of your knife-hand forearm. Immediately after your block stops the motion of his arm, pull your hand back slightly and snap it downward to cut his forearm. If you blocked a low cut or thrust, cut upward to get his arm.

Practicing drills helps you develop timing, reflexes, and technique, but in a relatively controlled context. Knife sparring, however, will give you a taste of what it's like to try to cut your opponent while he's trying to cut you. The commercial rubber training knives discussed earlier can be used to safely spar full contact. An alternative is to use foam rubber shin guards folded in half lengthwise and held with adhesive tape. You can also make your own sparring knives by folding and taping a section of foam rubber typewriter pad (the black rubber pads that sit under typewriters). Whatever type of practice knife you choose, before you begin sparring, make sure you wear a pair of shop goggles to protect your eyes, as even a rubber knife can cause serious damage to an eye.

To integrate your free-hand striking into your sparring sessions, get some boxing gloves to wear on your free hand. The hand protectors made for martial arts sparring are even better, since they have open palms and allow you to grab as well as punch.

The scenarios for knife sparring are limited only by the imagination. You should strive, however, to make them as realistic as possible and avoid turning them into a sporting competition. Although prolonged sparring sessions allow you time to polish your skills and certainly should have a place in your training schedule, most real knife fights are brief encounters. As such, sparring sessions consisting of many brief exchanges are more beneficial to developing practical knife-fighting skills and *a realistic attitude* concerning the risks of knife fighting. If you don't get used to the idea that you can get cut five or six times before you slip in your own killing blow, you'll be in for a rude surprise the first time you go at it with a real blade. The ultimate form of sparring is to practice reacting to unrehearsed street-style knife ambushes and quick exchanges, ending each when a telling blow is landed by either party. Like real street attacks, sparring sessions should not be limited to knife versus knife scenarios. Toy baseball bats, plastic chain (sold in garden supply stores), and other similar items can also be used to simulate typical weapons you might face on the street.

Although it may seem that practicing responses to attacks in a training environment could never duplicate the real thing, with a little imagination, you can come damned close. Being aware of what's going on around you on the street will alert you to potential attacks and allow you as much lead time as you would have in a training session. Just remember to keep it realistic. Go at your partner hard as if you were attacking him for real. It's also a good idea to practice in a variety of settings to get used to moving on different types of terrain and around various types of obstacles. Practice in street clothes, too, since an attacker probably won't give you the luxury of changing into a pair of sweats before he tries to cut you.

Since sparring action is often fast and furious, it can be difficult to tell who cut whom where. One way to keep track is to use chalk or stamp pad ink to mark the edge of your practice blade. When it's all over, look for the marks on your body and your partner's and figure out who came out on top. Recently, a rubber practice knife specifically designed for this type of sparring was introduced. It's called the MeKong Delta Knife and consists of a rubber knife body with a canvas wick material sewn along the blade edge to hold chalk or water-based paint. At $19.95 a piece, they're not cheap, but if you're serious about your training, the cost may not bother you.

If you're really ambitious and have access to, or are willing to purchase, fencing or kendo equipment, you can spar full force with wooden knives. A fencing face mask, body protector, and gloves will protect you from being seriously injured by hard contact with a wooden knife. It will not be a painless experience, however. As such, it adds a bit more realism than sparring with rubber knives since the element of pain will definitely be there. Kendo (Japanese fencing with wooden mock samurai swords) equipment is a bit bulkier than Western fencing gear, but it provides better protection and makes the experience safe and painless. The advantage of sparring with equipment, in addition to the added realism of using your practice knife with full power, is that you can also apply many free-hand strikes, kicks, and other body weapon techniques with full power.

To be really effective with your fighting knife, you must practice using it in a combative application. You must know its balance and how it moves when you execute the slashes and thrusts now in your arsenal of techniques. You must also know how it feels to hit a solid target with your knife. That will let you know instantly if your grip was correct and if you really struck a target with power.

Obviously I'm not recommending sparring with live blades. However, you can easily construct practice targets that allow you to practice some real cutting with your fighting knife.

The first type of target is used to practice meets, passes, and follows with real contact. To make this target, get a broom handle or piece of dowel rod about 1 inch thick and about 3 or 4 feet long. Now get a few corrugated cardboard boxes and cut them open so you have some long strips of cardboard about 18 inches wide. With a staple gun, staple one edge of the cardboard to the length of dowel rod so the end of the cardboard and the end of the dowel are flush. Now roll the cardboard tightly around the dowel until if forms a bundle about 5 or 6 inches in diameter and secure it with heavy adhesive tape.

To use this target, have your training partner swing it at you as if it were an opponent's knife arm. Using a real blade, practice all your defensive responses, cutting the cardboard roll as if it were an attacker's forearm. Use a safety check with your free hand in conjunction with each meet, pass, and follow, but be careful not to let that sharp blade anywhere near your partner. Practicing like this lets you feel the impact of hitting a solid target with your knife and forces you to do your safety checks carefully to avoid cutting yourself with your own blade. Because of the momentum that can be developed with this target, prolonged practice can be hard on your knife. As such, it is recommended that this practice be reserved mostly for straight-bladed knives, not folders. If you really want to practice with a folder, go a bit light on the contact, since the stick can cause damage to the locking mechanism of your knife. If you don't have a training partner, it is also possible to make this type of target and mount it so you can practice solo.

To practice your cuts, thrusts, and knife withdrawals with a real blade, a bale of hay makes a great target. Set it up on a crate or stack several bales to make a target high enough for realistic practice. Be careful not to nick your knife edge on the baling wire or else replace the wire with rope before you start cutting.

If you can't get hay bales, a good practice target can also be made from layers of corrugated cardboard. Make a stack several inches thick and tape it together with duct or filament tape. Then hang it from a wall, tree, or other sturdy support. To practice thrusting and cutting accurately, draw targets to aim at on the cardboard. By putting a number of targets in various locations on the cardboard, you can practice thrusting at and cutting targets in your peripheral vision. Rather than concentrating on each specific point, focus your gaze on the entire target and use your peripheral vision, along with the guiding ability of your extended thumb, to help you hit the targets. This helps prevent telegraphing your intentions with your eyes when you fight for real and develops your overall awareness.

Cardboard targets are also ideal for practicing knife withdrawal techniques. After thrusting into the target, do a comma cut and simultaneous push off to free your blade. This will not only give you a realistic idea of the force required to withdraw a deeply imbedded knife, close examination of the cardboard when you're done will show you the devastation a comma cut can cause.

Solo practice should also be included in your training regimen. This training is basically shadow boxing with a knife. It should include all the cuts and thrusts in your arsenal, combined with empty hand strikes, kicks, and anything else you might use in a real fight. Don't just throw your techniques randomly. Imagine actual attacks that someone might throw at you, visualize gaps in his defenses, and use offensive tactics that would take advantage of these gaps. As with all training, the more realistic it is, the better it will prepare you for a real fight. Solo practice is also a good way to perfect your safety checks to avoid cutting yourself with your own blade. Start slow and develop speed after you're confident with the various movements.

One type of training that is often neglected by knife fighters is practicing with your weak hand. It is possible that your strong hand will be cut and disabled during a fight. If this happens, you need to be able to continue the fight with your other hand. Weak hand skills can also come in handy even when your strong hand is fully functional. One example was already described in the chapter on counterdefenses: switching your knife to the weak hand in the event that your strong-hand knife wrist is grabbed. If attacked while seated in a vehicle, it might be an advantage or a necessity to employ your knife with your weak hand. Switching your knife from one hand to another can also give you the advantage of surprise in a stand-up knife fight. The technique of doing this does not resemble that shown in the 1950s street-gang movies, however. The hands are brought close together to pass the knife. It is *not* tossed from hand to hand. This tactic is risky, at best, and should be used sparingly. Weak-hand training, however, should be a part of every practice session. The drills and sparring scenarios you use to develop your ability with your primary hand can be just as beneficial to your weak-hand skills.

Applied Knife Fighting and the Real World

Most of this book has been dedicated to explaining basic principles of knife fighting and the technique of applying a knife as an offensive and defensive weapon. In most cases, the starting scenario has been that of a stereotypical knife fight: you and your opponent both armed with blades and facing each other head on. However, as I mentioned in Chapter 1, this scenario is not the most likely one you'll encounter. A more typical scene would be an ambush. Your opponent will come at you without warning, armed with anything from a blade to a brick. He will not issue a threat to allow you time to pull your blade before the conflict starts. He will be on top of you, cutting or hitting before you know it.

What can you do to prepare for such an attack? Well, first, make the conscious decision that you are going to carry a knife and use it to defend your life if attacked. Then do your best to master the techniques and principles demonstrated in the preceding chapters and keep practicing them regularly. Don't think that by just having a knife in your pocket and reading about knife fighting that you'll be ready to take on a determined attacker.

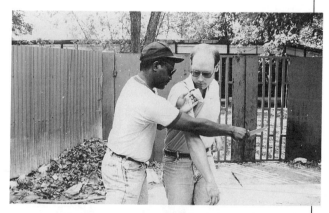
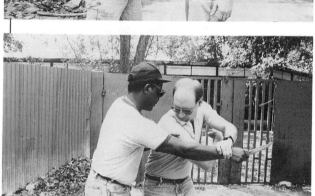

Maintaining a critical awareness of your surroundings is the key to recognizing an attack before it happens. No matter how hard you try, though, sometimes you may have little time to react. In such cases, you must defend yourself unarmed or with whatever is at hand first to buy time to draw your blade. Here an attacker tries a surprise stabbing assault. The defender pivots to clear his body from the line of attack and deflects the knife arm with the outside of his forearm. He then controls the knife hand with his free hand and strikes with a powerful hammerfist to the groin. With the attacker temporarily stunned, our hero pushes his way and steps back to create distance so he can draw his own blade to continue the fight if necessary. If possible, his next act should be to vacate the area.

The movements described in this book will work against attacks with practically any type of hand-held weapon or against an empty-handed attack. They need only be adjusted to take into account the characteristics of the attacking weapon. For example, a baseball bat or a chain will circumvent a block administered to the weapon hand and still strike with force. As such, a meet is not advisable unless it is used during the initial or final phases of the swing when the weapon's momentum is at its lowest point. Realistic practice with a variety of simulated weapons will teach you how to react properly.

In addition to practicing the tactics of using the knife after it is drawn, think carefully about the type of knife you will carry and how you will carry it. Decide if you want the convenience and innocuousness of a folder or if you want the strength and speed of a straight-bladed boot knife. Also think about the legal consequences of carrying a particular blade in your area and how much hassle you'd be willing to endure if a cop discovers your knife. Then look at the way you dress, both day to day and on special occasions. Where could a knife be carried most comfortably yet still be instantly accessible? Are all your clothes the same basic style? Do you wear different clothing during different seasons of the year? Do you spend a lot of time seated in a vehicle? (The frequency of attacks on people seated in their vehicles is increasing, so you must be able to draw your blade from practically any position.)

The idea is to settle on one standard place to carry your knife and stick with it, regardless of your style of dress. Carrying a folder in your pocket one day and a straight blade in your boot the next will not allow you to develop the conditioned reflex needed to draw your knife under pressure. If it's always in the same place, you can, with sufficient practice, develop the ability to retrieve your knife automatically and with great speed when confronted with a threat.

If you carry a folder, you'll also need to learn to open it quickly under stress. In addition to the conventional two-handed methods, you should also master a few one-handed opening techniques so you can still get your knife into action if one of your arms is immobilized or disabled. One-handed opening techniques also have a definite psychological impact on an attacker, though their intimidating effect should not be overestimated.

Once you've learned to carry, draw, handle, and fight with your knife, you need to learn what to do to defend against an attack barehanded. In the event that you are taken totally by surprise and are unable to have your knife ready to go when you need it, an unarmed or

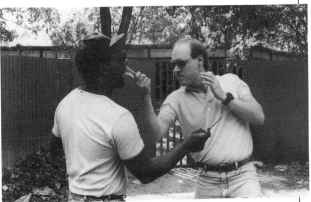

The last resort in a knife fight is to take a cut. If you have no other choice but to be cut, at least minimize the damage you'll suffer and give back more than you take! Caught by surprise by an inside slash, the knife fighter takes the cut on the outside of his forearm and counters with an immediate thrust to the eye. Obviously, this is a tactic you'll only want to use once in a fight.

improvised defense will keep you alive and allow you to buy enough time to draw your blade and mount a more effective defense.

Unarmed defenses against a knife, while not impossible, are risky. The odds of getting cut are extremely high. As such, your main objective should be to get out of the way of your opponent's blade (or other weapon) and move far enough out of range to draw your knife. This can be done by angling and using defensive footwork alone, if necessary. Against thrusts to the body, a quick twist of the hips and slight shift of body weight can take you completely out of the line of attack. This movement is ideal for close quarters, since it requires no stepping or change of foot position. The hip twist can also be combined with a straight arm deflection with the outside of your lead forearm. As your body pivots, extend your lead arm slightly away from your body with the fingers pointed down and the outside of the forearm facing out. Your forearm can be used to deflect a thrust, giving you an extra margin of safety in your defense.

A better solution to a surprise knife attack than a passive evasion or deflection is to combine the evasive footwork with *effective* strikes and kicks, namely finger pokes to the eyes and kicks to the knee joint. An eye gouge need not be powerful to be effective, and the natural human reaction to cover one's eyes with the hands when they are injured can mean an instant disarm.

A kick to the knee joint also doesn't require much force to do a lot of damage. The knee is vulnerable because it joins the two longest bones of the body. Any pressure to the center third of the leg therefore exerts tremendous leverage against that joint. A well-placed kick can put your opponent down and possibly out of the fight altogether. At the very least, it will buy you time to arm yourself and limit his mobility for the rest of the fight.

Although I don't discourage the formal study of the martial arts to develop your unarmed fighting abilities, the knife defenses taught in most styles of martial arts simply don't work against a realistic knife attack. The only martial arts that deal with knife attacks realistically are those that also emphasize the combative use of the knife, namely the Filipino martial arts and Indonesian *pencak-silat*. If in doubt, explain your objective to your prospective martial arts instructor and ask him to demonstrate his style's knife defenses to you in private. This keeps him from losing face in front of his students and avoids the typical macho challenge thing. If he goes for it, judge the techniques for yourself and see if you think they would really work against a skilled knife fighter. If he tells you that those techniques are for advanced students only or that you wouldn't appreciate their effectiveness without the benefit of fundamental training in his style, don't waste your time.

The preferred method of defense against ambush attacks, however, is to use improvised weapons to slow your attacker down, distract him, or injure him to give you time to bring your blade into action. The number of improvised weapons that can be used in the event of an attack is virtually endless. Anything that can be picked up in the hand can be thrown at your attacker to buy you time and distance. Dirt, ashes, rocks, coins, keys, or other small objects thrown in your attacker's face can distract or temporarily blind him. Larger objects like chairs, garbage cans, boxes, etc., can be picked up and chucked at him with both hands, allowing you precious seconds to draw your blade and prepare your defense.

Of course to be able to take any kind of defensive action, armed or unarmed, you'll have to realize early enough that you're being attacked to do something about it. That means being aware of what's going on around you at all times and being able to pick up on the signs that precede an attack. You might think that some of the signs, like being set up or stalked by an attacker, might be obvious; however, depending upon the skill and cunning of your attacker, they can be surprisingly subtle. It would be impossible to describe all the indicators here, but one of the key things to look for is the positioning of people around you. Be wary of people trying to flank you, move behind you, place you between them, or cut off your avenues of escape. Look for people whose hands are cupped or unnaturally stiff, like something is held in them, or concealed from view behind the back or in a pocket. Most importantly, don't let anyone get too close to you, where they might be able to move on you before you can react. If someone starts to move close, try to position your back against a wall and put something between you and him as an obstacle to any advance. At the very least, tell him to back off, so you can have enough distance between you to react if he makes a move. If he doesn't listen and keeps coming, draw your blade and prepare for all hell to break loose.

One tactic that may come naturally in a fight but is taught formally in many traditional martial arts is screaming. A sharp scream prior to executing an offensive action can startle your opponent and leave him unable to react for a second or two, which is all the time you need to poke a few holes in him. When executed concurrent with an attack, a scream can give you greater strength and confidence. Obviously, screaming also can draw attention to your plight and possibly bring help. Finally, done convincingly, prolonged screaming can make your opponent believe that you are mentally unstable. Most attackers, even daring ones, won't mess with crazy people.

Another trick is to talk to your opponent to create an opening for an attack. Given the situation, he will be on edge and will most likely have preconceived ideas as to how the scenario will progress. By talking to him and especially by asking him questions, you can force

him to think about things that didn't figure into his original plan. While he's thinking, his reaction time will be dramatically slower, so ask him a question and then immediately cut him.

There's no ignoring the fact that knife fighting is a dirty, dangerous business. The destructive power of a knife on human tissue is awesome. If you don't believe it, spend an evening or two at the emergency room of a large urban hospital. Odds are you'll get to see first hand what sharp blades can do to people. With those images in mind, learn the material in this book and practice it until it becomes second nature. The skill you develop will give you the confidence and ability to defend your life with a knife and the judgment to avoid having to.

No matter how proficient you may become at fighting with a knife, this is still the best solution when confronted with the prospect of a knife fight.

Suggestions for Further Study

There are a number of knife-fighting books out on the market, ranging from reprints of World War II training manuals to recently published works. There are also several videos on this subject. Although I don't necessarily agree with the teachings professed in some of these, I have learned something from every one of them. As the saying goes, a little knowledge can be a dangerous thing, so if you're serious about developing your knife skills, read and watch everything you can get your hands on. Try what each book or video has to offer and see if the techniques work for you. If they do, add them to your arsenal. If they don't, figure out why they don't work and remember their specific faults and weaknesses. That way, if you run into somebody who happens to fight that way, you will have the edge.

Of the books and videos available, the ones that should be at the top of your list are mentioned below.

• *Cold Steel* by John Styers, Paladin Press. This is a reprint of the classic World War II training text and probably the most authoritative book you'll find on military knife fighting. It may not include much that will convince you to change your technique, but no knife-fighting library would be complete without it.

• *Combat Use of the Double-Edged Fighting Knife* by Col. Rex Applegate. The latest work by one of the legendary figures in the close-combat arena, this book features highlights of Colonel Applegate's knife-fighting method and selected commentary on knife design, practice targets, and other related subjects.

• *Green Beret Knife Fighting* by Michael Janich and James Webb, Panther Productions. This series of videos on knife fighting contains much, but not all, of the information contained in this book. The title comes from the fact that Jim Webb is a former Green Beret and that such an association translates into good marketing. Actually, the knife-fighting system taught in these videos has nothing to do with the Special Forces per se, but it is without a doubt the most comprehensive instructional video series ever presented on knife fighting and knife throwing. As you may have guessed, I recommend it highly.

• *Knives, Knife Fighting, and Related Hassles* by Marc "Animal" MacYoung, Paladin Press. This book, as well as the video *Surviving a Street Knife Fight* by the same author, provides great insight into the grim realities of knife encounters on the street. These works also contain some great comments on the psychology of knife encounters and are highly recommended.

• *Put 'Em Down, Take 'Em Out: Knife Fighting Techniques from Folsom Prison* by Don Pentecost, Paladin Press. The knife-fighting method described in this book was developed in one of the most violent environments on earth. It is therefore best suited to that environment and other all-out, kill-or-be-killed scenarios. It also gives you an insight into prison knife fighting, which can be invaluable if you ever find yourself facing an alumnus of this particular school of hard knocks.

• *Surviving Edged Weapons* by Calibre Press. This video is primarily targeted at law enforcement officers to make them aware of the dangers of edged-weapon attacks and to use proper armed police tactics to prevent or thwart them. It doesn't offer much in the way of unarmed defenses or knife-to-knife tactics, but provides excellent information concerning actual street knife attacks and grisly video evidence of their results. The reenactments of actual attacks that are shown in this video are an excellent source of inspiration for realistic sparring scenarios.